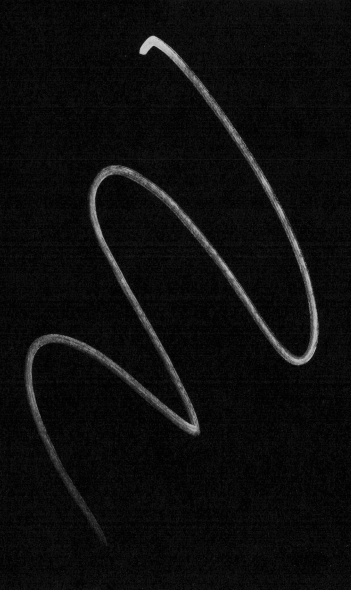

"No biblical or theological subject captivates my heart and stimulates my mind more than the glory of Christ. One day every knee will bow at the mention of his name. If you want to understand why (and have your own heart humbled, filled with gratitude, and aroused to worship), nourish your soul with this simple yet profound overview of who Jesus is and what he has accomplished."

John MacArthur, Pastor, Grace Community Church; President, The Master's College and Seminary; speaker, *Grace to You*

"As Christians, we find it easy to talk about God's work in our communities and around the world. It's easy to describe our growth in Christ and what we are learning from him. But how many of us simply delight in talking about Jesus? The art of contemplating the loveliness of Christ—and infusing those admirations into everyday conversation—is a dying discipline. But in *Name above All Names*, my friends Alistair Begg and Sinclair Ferguson invite us to meditate afresh on our wonderful Savior and all that makes him beautiful and praiseworthy. I highly recommend this remarkable volume!"

Joni Eareckson Tada, founder and CEO, Joni and Friends International Disability Center

"Who is Jesus? There is no more important question human beings can face. Alistair Begg and Sinclair Ferguson provide a wealth of knowledge about Christ by looking at how Christ is presented in the New Testament through a collection of exquisite images. Every Christian will celebrate this book as these two gifted authors bring us into an even deeper understanding of who Christ is and who he is for us."

R. Albert Mohler Jr., President, The Southern Baptist Theological Seminary

"You can't have too many good books about the person and work of Jesus Christ. And this is a great book. Alistair Begg and Sinclair Ferguson handle the most important doctrines of the faith with clarity, fidelity, pastoral insight, and good humor. New Christians, non-Christians, and long-time Christians will benefit from these superb expositions."

Kevin DeYoung, Senior Pastor, University Reformed Church, East Lansing, Michigan

"For all those who, like me, have spent a lifetime in church hearing the Bible stories but have only begun to grasp the central story of the Bible, *Name above All Names* winsomely and clearly connects the dots. Two wise guides help us to see Jesus throughout the Scriptures—from the promise of his coming as the seed of the woman in Genesis to the promise of his coming again as the Lamb on the throne in Revelation."

Nancy Guthrie, Bible teacher; author, Seeing Jesus in the Old Testament series

NAME

above All

NAMES

NAME

above All

NAMES

ALISTAIR BEGG AND
SINCLAIR B. FERGUSON

WHEATON, ILLINOIS

LB		23	22	21	20	19	18	17	16	15	14	13
15	14	13	12	11	10	9	8	7	6	5	4	3	2	1

To
Derek Prime—
Christian
Pastor
Example
Encourager
Friend
With Affection and Gratitude

Contents

Preface

This book, as its title suggests, is a brief exposition of what Christians often refer to as "the person and work of Christ." Its focus is on some of the different ways in which the Bible portrays Christ's identity and describes his ministry. The chapters are by no means exhaustive. They cover only seven of the many descriptions of Jesus found in the Bible, and none of those descriptions is treated exhaustively. So these pages are meant as a taster, a beginning exploration. Our joint prayer is that they will help some who are not yet Christians, be an eye-opener to those who already are, serve as an encouragement for mature believers, and be a pleasure for all who love Christ.

We cannot claim that this is a "special" book. But there are two special things about it that may lend interest to reading it.

For one thing, it is a concrete expression of a friendship, begun in the 1970s when we were both very young ministers in Scotland, that now spans five decades. We were born and lived the first years of our lives in the same city. We knew the same places, were taught the same psalms, hymns, and spiritual songs, heard the same preachers, developed a network of mutual friends, and, yes, even supported the same soccer team and played on some of the same golf courses. We both came to minister in the United States within a few months of each other, in 1983.

Of course we are different personalities and live within our own worlds (one has become an American citizen, the other hasn't; one plays the guitar, the other doesn't; one is a Baptist, the other a Presbyterian; one lives in Cleveland, the other in Columbia; and so on). We both have our own circle of friends as well as intersecting circles of friends. But over these many years we have enjoyed the kind of friendship, esteem, and affection for one another that has made us feel we are brothers. One of us never had a brother; the other lost his brother. So in part this book and its theme are expressions of our joint gratitude to the Savior in whom we have enjoyed such friendship and the love for his people we share in common.

But in addition, *Name above All Names* gives us the opportunity to do something we have talked about over the years: express in some tangible way our joint gratitude for Derek Prime, who has been to us model pastor, friend, and encourager. That would be true especially for Alistair who served with Derek Prime at Charlotte Chapel, Edinburgh, from 1974–1976. Our sense of gratitude for the measure of Christ-centeredness and Christlikeness we have seen displayed in his life and ministry makes it very natural for us to dedicate to him this little book on our Savior and Lord.

The material in these pages began to come together in its present form as we prepared for a conference at The Second Presbyterian Church in Memphis, Tennessee. We are indebted to that congregation and to its senior minister, Sandy Willson, for giving us the opportunity to serve them together and to share some of the material here in spoken form. We are also indebted to Mrs. Eve Huffman for the secretarial help without which this project would never have been completed.

We hope these pages will encourage, instruct, refresh, and challenge every reader. In order to make it more practically helpful to those with only a beginning knowledge of the Bible, we have included references to the Bible passages or texts to which we refer. These references are in footnotes so that the book may be read without the constant interruption of bracketed material.

We ask one favor from our readers. Standing in various pulpits in our native land of Scotland we have often seen words visible to the preacher but hidden from the congregation: "Sir, we wish to see Jesus" (John 12:21). We ask you to make that your prayer as you begin to turn these pages.

Alistair Begg
Sinclair B. Ferguson

1

Jesus Christ, the Seed of the Woman

Jesus Christ has been given the name above all names.[1] The names assigned him begin in Genesis and end in Revelation. Taken together they express the incomparable character of Jesus Christ our Savior and Lord. Reflecting on them better prepares us to respond to the exhortations of Scripture, to focus our gaze upon him, and to meditate on how great he is.

Being able to think long and lovingly about the Lord Jesus is a dying art. The disciplines required to reflect on him for a prolonged period of time and to be captivated by him have been relegated to a secondary place in contemporary Christian life. Action, rather than meditation, is the order of the day. Sadly, too often that action is not suffused with the grace and power of Christ.

How different is the example of the apostle Paul—for whom "to live is Christ"[2]—or the author of the letter to the Hebrews, who urges us to "consider Jesus."[3]

We need to learn to recapture such Christ-centeredness in our activist, busy age. Many of us are by nature too impatient. The most common tools of life, used on a daily basis—our computers and all of our technology—simply increase that impatience.

[1] Phil. 2:9.
[2] Phil. 1:21.
[3] Heb. 3:1.

It can only do us good, then, to spend the few hours it will take to read these pages focused on and riveted to the person and the work of our Lord Jesus Christ.

The beginning, as Julie Andrews reminds us, "is a very good place to start." Genesis is the book of beginnings. There we find the first hint of the coming of a redeemer. He is the Seed of the woman.

In the Garden

The title of this chapter is drawn from words God spoke in the garden of Eden. He addressed the Serpent that had just successfully tempted Adam and Eve into sin:

> I will put enmity between you and the woman,
>   and between your offspring [seed] and her offspring [seed];
> he shall bruise your head,
>   and you shall bruise his heel.[4]

The context is a familiar one.

God has put Adam and Eve into a beautiful garden. Every tree in that garden is good to look at and its fruit tastes delicious. But there is one tree in the garden about which God has said, "Of the tree of the knowledge of good and evil you shall not eat, for in the day you eat of it you will die."[5]

The point, apparently, was not that there was anything inherently poisonous about this particular tree. In fact, it is described in exactly the same terms as every other tree. It does not bear ugly fruit with a poisonous aroma. No. The distinctive feature of this tree is *what God has said about it*. For the all-generous God, who has given Adam and Eve everything in the garden to enjoy, has also said to them:

> Now, prove your love for me, show your trust in me and your
> obedience to me as a generous God, not because you can tell

---

[4] Gen. 3:15.
[5] Gen. 2:17.

the difference between that tree and any other tree, but simply because I, as your Father, have told you, "Trust me and obey me" with respect to this one tree.

It is a call to the life of faith that runs from the beginning of the Bible to its end:

> Trust and obey, for there's no other way
> To be happy in Jesus, but to trust and obey.[6]

But then the Serpent appeared singing a different song:

> Trust me and obey, for there's no other way
> To be happy without God, except—do what I say.

"Did God set you in this garden full of all these glorious trees, and all this delicious fruit, and then say, 'You are not to eat of the fruit of *any* of the trees'?"

Of course, Eve tried to argue with him, but she failed and was eventually drawn in to his scheme. She assessed the significance of the tree through her eyes rather than through her ears! Instead of listening to *what God said about it*, she thought about it only in terms of *what she could see on it*. After all, it looked delicious as well as attractive. She had not grasped the divine principle: believers "see" with their ears, not with their eyes, by listening to God's Word![7]

This, of course, is always the Serpent's trick.[8]

In addition, what better way to bring about the fall of Adam other than—as Eve herself later admitted—by deceiving her and then employing her? Satan used the very best of God's gifts to Adam to gain leverage on him and to draw him into sin. And so, in turn, Adam brought the cosmos to ruin.

God comes and exposes the sinful pair. They make their pa-

---

[6] John H. Sammis, "Trust and Obey," 1887.
[7] King David was to make the same mistake (2 Sam. 11:1–2).
[8] See Josh. 7:18, 20–21; 2 Sam. 11:2 for further illustrations in the cases of Achan and David.

thetic excuses. The man blames the woman. The woman blames the Serpent.

Then God pronounces three words of judgment.[9]

1) There is a judgment on Adam related to his task of gardening and his calling to turn the whole world into a garden for God.

2) There is a judgment on Eve related particularly to childbearing and to her attitude toward her husband.

3) There is a judgment on the Serpent.

Amazingly this judgment on the Serpent contains a seed of glorious gospel hope:

> I will put enmity between you and the woman,
>   and between your offspring [seed] and her offspring [seed];
> he shall bruise your head,
>   and you shall bruise his heel.[10]

Emmaus Road Reading

When we trace the way the Old Testament develops this theme, we are, in a sense, trying to catch up with Jesus himself as he talked with two of his disciples on the road to Emmaus on the afternoon of his resurrection.[11] We are trying to overhear what he said.

The disciples were confused, bewildered, and distressed because of Jesus' death. He pointed them to the Scriptures: "Do you not see how these Scriptures show that the Messiah would suffer and die and rise again and enter his kingdom and then extend that kingdom to the whole world?"

Apparently they didn't.

How much we would love to have been there with an iPhone or a Blackberry set to RECORD to be able to play back all the Old Testament passages to which he drew their attention. He clearly had them memorized! Presumably he simply worked his way through

---

[9] Gen. 3:15–17.
[10] Gen. 3:15.
[11] Luke 24:13–35.

them on that short journey.[12] Later, for a period of several weeks, he kept coming back to the disciples and showing them all the ways in which the Old Testament pointed to him.[13]

When our Lord Jesus did this—and whenever he still does it through his Word and by his Spirit—three things happen:

- First, he provides an *exposition* of the Scriptures.
- Second, he brings *illumination* to the mind.
- Third, he creates a *passion* for himself in the heart.

"Did not our hearts burn within us while he talked to us on the road, while he opened to us the Scriptures?"[14] That was the reaction of the two disciples when he left them.

This is the function of any Bible study. It is what we want to happen whenever we read what the Bible has to teach us about Jesus. We read or hear the Scriptures, and we look to the Holy Spirit to illumine them. When he does, our hearts burn within us. They are "strangely warmed" (to use John Wesley's words). If we have once experienced this kind of heart burning, we want our hearts to burn like that again and again with love for the Savior and his teaching.

If that is to happen, there is no better place to start than where we suspect Jesus made his beginning, in Genesis 3:15—here in this promise of the conflict between the two seeds.

The antagonists are first described as the seed of the woman and the seed of the Serpent. But the climax of the conflict is destined to be more personal and individual—between the seed of the woman and the Serpent itself. The final evil antagonist is no longer the seed of the Serpent but the Serpent itself. Implicitly, then, the final seed of the woman is also an individual. Each would crush the other. But whereas the Serpent would crush only the heel of the

---

[12] Luke says, "He interpreted to them in all the Scriptures the things concerning himself" (Luke 24:27; see also 24:44–47).

[13] Acts 1:3.

[14] Luke 24:32.

seed of the woman, the seed of the woman would crush the head of the Serpent—a blow that would prove fatal.

If we were to give you a 3x5 blank card, inviting you to answer the question, "For what reason did the Son of God appear?" what would your answer be? Here is the apostle John's answer:

> The reason the Son of God appeared was to destroy the works of the devil.[15]

That is the very first dimension of the gospel recorded in the Bible. John saw the prophecy of Genesis 3 fulfilled in our Redeemer Jesus Christ. When Christ appeared, he came to undo what the Serpent had done. By his life and ministry and ultimately through his death and resurrection, he destroyed all the works of the Devil.

How do these words illumine the ministry of our Lord Jesus Christ?

When we think about salvation, we use words like *forgiveness* and *justification*—and rightly so. But notice that there is no mention in Genesis 3:15 of forgiveness or justification. Does that not matter? Indeed it does! But God's words here place all the emphasis on conflict ("I will put enmity . . .") and therefore on our need to be delivered from bondage to the Evil One so that we are no longer the prisoners of "the prince of the power of the air, the spirit that is now at work in the sons of disobedience."[16]

And so these words, almost at the beginning of Genesis, give us an important insight into the whole message of the Bible. It is a library of books that traces an ages-long cosmic conflict between the two "seeds."

The Protevangelium

Genesis 3:15 has long been referred to as the "Protevangelium," the first announcement of the good news of the gospel. It contains the

---

[15] 1 John 3:8.
[16] Eph. 2:2.

earliest promise of Christ's coming—a prophecy that his appearance will be the climax of an extended conflict. Notice how this is expressed:

a) I will put enmity between you and the woman,
b) and between your offspring and her offspring;
c) he shall bruise your head, and you shall bruise his heel.

- In the first statement (a) God declares enmity between the Serpent and the woman.
- In the second statement (b) God indicates that this will continue beyond the lifetime of Eve and involve the offspring (seed) of the Serpent and the seed of the woman.
- In the third statement (c) God says that the enmity will come to a climax when the offspring ("he") of the woman bruises (or crushes) the head of the Serpent. The conflict ends in the victory of the seed of the woman.

So there is a development in this verse, from enmity between two individuals (the Serpent and Eve), to enmity between two family lines (their offspring), to a final dénouement: the woman's offspring or seed (singular) will crush the head of the Serpent.

Satan?

There is no reference to Satan in Genesis 3. But when the rest of the Scriptures reflect on what happened there, it is clear that behind the Serpent stands the figure of Satan.

Paul echoes Genesis 3:15 when he tells the Christians in Rome that "the God of peace will soon crush Satan under your feet."[17] He is picking up this ancient promise and applying it to the Christians in Rome. The implication is that the Serpent in Genesis 3 is the mouthpiece of Satan, and that the conflict referred to there has now come to a climax. Christ overcomes him—and therefore so shall we.

---

[17] Rom. 16:20.

This is even more vividly expressed in the book of Revelation. Revelation 12 gives us a dramatic picture of this ages-long conflict reaching its climax. John sees a great red dragon that devours humanity. This is the "ancient serpent, who is called the devil and Satan, the deceiver of the whole world."[18] Having spiritually devoured so many from the human race, the Serpent of Eden has grown into a large dragon.

In fact, the apocalyptic vision of Revelation 12 is almost like a movie version of Genesis 3:15. We are invited to watch, in dramatic, high-definition, Technicolor with special effects, the prophesied ongoing conflict between the seed of the woman and the seed of the Serpent and its final outcome.[19]

This is the underlying plotline of the whole of the Bible. It appears in embryo in the very next chapter of the book of Genesis. One brother (Cain) is in conflict with another brother (Abel) because the latter's sacrifice was acceptable to God.[20] Jealousy and murder result as the seed of the Serpent (Cain), seeks to destroy the seed of the woman (Abel).

The same plotline makes its way through the tower of Babel as man seeks to build his kingdom over against God's. But in sovereign power God pulls down that kingdom and destroys its unity.[21] This is also the story of Egypt against Israel.[22] It is the story of Goliath against David.[23] It is the story of Babylon against Jerusalem, of Nebuchadnezzar against Daniel.[24] It is the story of Satan against Jesus,[25] and of Pontius Pilate and Herod seeking to destroy the Savior.[26] It is the story that runs through the Gospels and be-

---

[18] Rev. 12:9.
[19] Elsewhere, by implication, the New Testament makes this same identification of the Serpent with Satan: John 8:44b.
[20] Gen. 4:1ff.
[21] Gen. 11:1–9.
[22] Exodus 1–12.
[23] 1 Sam. 17:10, 45.
[24] Dan. 1:1ff.
[25] Matt. 16:21–23; Luke 4:1–13, 28–29, 31–37; 22:53; John 12:27–33; 13:2, 21–32.
[26] Acts 4:23–28.

yond. The Jews seek to destroy Jesus during his ministry: "You are of your father the devil," he says.[27] It is the story of how the enmity then turns on the Christian church.[28]

Thus the story of the ages is beginning to unfold here already in Genesis 3:15.

Ongoing Conflict

We need to remember this conflict when we come to read the Gospels. It is a major underlying theme in the life and ministry of the Lord Jesus. Its presence runs through every page of the story. The Gospels are the story of Jesus' conflict with the seed of the Serpent—whether in the form of demons, or in the inciting of hostility against him, or in his efforts to conscript into his service Jesus' disciples Peter and Judas. In the terse summary language of the aged John: "The reason the Son of God appeared was to destroy the works of the devil."[29]

And so from the beginning to the very end, from the garden of Eden turned into a desert because of sin, until in Revelation 21 and 22 when that desert is turned back into a garden, the whole of the Bible is the story of this conflict. It was promised to last throughout the ages until Christ came, and then, in his ministry, it enters its critical phase.

The New Testament reflects this in many different ways.

Remember how Paul says that when the time was fully come, God sent his Son. He describes Jesus in two arresting phrases, "born of woman, born under the law."[30] "Born of woman"—is he echoing Genesis 3:15? Surely, for lineage elsewhere in Scripture is traced through the male line.[31] But God had said, "The *seed of the woman* will crush the head of the serpent." Paul is, as it were, say-

---

[27] John 8:44.
[28] Acts 7:54–8:3.
[29] 1 John 3:8.
[30] Gal. 4:4.
[31] See, for example, Gen. 5:1; 6:9; 10:1; Matt. 1:1–17; Luke 4:23–38.

ing to us, "Now do you see in the incarnation *who* the seed—the one born of—the woman actually is? It is none other than the Lord Jesus Christ."

Could this be the reason why the Lord Jesus addresses his mother Mary as the "woman"? He does that in two very striking moments recorded exclusively in John's Gospel.

First, at the wedding Jesus was attending in Cana of Galilee, he responds to Mary's insistence that he "do something" about an impending disaster. The wine was running out. But Jesus answers: "*Woman*, what does this have to do with me? My hour has not yet come." But shortly afterwards he turned water into wine—his first miracle; his first display of his glory![32]

Later, during the last hour or so of his life, Jesus again addresses his mother as "woman." He is about to finish his work on earth. In that work God "disarmed the rulers and authorities and put them to open shame."[33] As he does so, he turns to John and commits his mother Mary into his care. And then he says to her, "*Woman*, behold, your son!"[34]

Commentators have always found it difficult to explain the precise nuance of Jesus' words. They seem to jar a little. After all, when did you last address your mother in this impersonal form? And if you did, what did she say? Did she remind you who she is? To our ears there is something abrasive about such language when used by a son of his loving mother. Some commentators go to great lengths to say, "Now, there is no tension here. This is a very normal thing for Jesus to say."

But is it? This style of address between a son and his mother does not appear elsewhere in the Gospels. Could there be a deeper reason why John records this language at both the beginning and the end of Jesus' public ministry? Is he saying: "Don't you see what

---

[32] See John 2:1–11.
[33] Col. 2:15.
[34] John 19:26.

is happening here? Jesus sees he is *the seed of the woman* who would bruise the head of the Serpent." Is he simply reminding his mother of their God-given destinies? After all, John's Gospel teaches us that, on the cross of Calvary, our Lord Jesus Christ did, in fact, crush the head of the Serpent. "Now" he says, when Gentiles asked to see him, "Now is the judgment of this world; now will the ruler of this world be cast out."[35]

Jesus Meets the Enemy

Another passage in John's Gospel seems to fit in with this overall perspective, although it too is far from easy to interpret.

In the middle of our Lord's Farewell Discourse (John 13–17) he says to his disciples, "Rise, let us go from here [or, let us be going]" (14:31). But there is no indication in the text of any physical relocation or indeed of any movement at all. However, the language John uses here was employed outside of the New Testament in a military context, for marching against the enemy. Perhaps, then, Jesus is not saying, "Come on, let's move on from here," but rather, " In the light of all that I have been saying and all that is happening, it is time for us to march into the final conflict against the powers of darkness."[36] For, "this is [their] hour, and the power of darkness."[37] Whether the disciple band physically left the room at that point or not, Jesus was certainly entering enemy-occupied territory.

And so the Gospels seem to be saying to us: "Do you see in the ministry of the Lord Jesus how this promise of conflict is coming to a climactic point?"

Revelation 12 is a dramatic form of this promise of Genesis 3:15. In his vision, John sees that a child who will rule the nations

---

[35] John 12:31.
[36] See John 14:31. See C. H. Dodd, *The Interpretation of the Fourth Gospel* (Cambridge, UK: Cambridge University Press, 1953), 407–9.
[37] Luke 22:53.

is about to be born.[38] But a great dragon stands waiting for him to come from his mother's womb. The dragon means to devour the child. The dragon is explicitly identified with the Devil and the Serpent in Eden.[39] This is all too reminiscent of the vicious and cynical pogrom Herod mounted against the infants in the region of Bethlehem.[40] There was something deeply satanic about that attack, focused as it was on the person of the Lord Jesus Christ. The story of salvation is a wartime story.

The same realities come to expression in our Savior's temptation in the wilderness.[41]

The Second Adam Comes to the Fight

We sometimes make an elementary mistake when reading the temptation narratives. We assume that their chief purpose is to teach us about *our* temptations and how we should resist them.

True, our Lord's example of resisting his temptations does help us to withstand our temptations. But their point is not to say, "Jesus was tempted, and you are tempted just like him, so respond to temptation as he did." That would turn his temptations into a mere example for us to emulate. No—we are told that the Holy Spirit *led* Jesus, indeed "drove him," into the wilderness to be tempted.[42]

Jesus' temptations were not a series of unfortunate events that overtook him unexpectedly. They constitute an epic confrontation taking place within the divine strategy. What we see here is Jesus' work of conflict, victory, and salvation. He came face-to-face with Satan. He appeared as God's new man, the second Adam, to do what the old man, the first Adam, had failed to do. The question is:

---

[38] His language makes clear that he sees this child through the lens of Psalm 2:9. He is the promised messianic King.
[39] Rev. 12:9.
[40] Matt. 2:16–18.
[41] Matt. 4:1–11; Mark 1:12–13; Luke 4:1–13.
[42] "Led" is Luke's expression; "drove" is Mark's.

who will possess the kingdoms of this world? And how will God's kingdom be recovered and established? And the answer is that Jesus will repossess them in our name and for his Father's pleasure and glory. Satan will be crushed under foot!

> O loving wisdom of our God!
> When all was sin and shame,
> A Second Adam to the fight
> And to the rescue came.
>
> O wisest love! that flesh and blood,
> That did in Adam fail,
> Should strive afresh against the foe,
> Should strive and should prevail.[43]

This is why Jesus experienced such overwhelming weakness and hunger (in contrast to Adam, who enjoyed plenty). This is why he faced temptation in a wilderness (not like Adam, situated in a lovely and hospitable garden). This is why he was surrounded by wild animals (not, as Adam was, by pliant, obedient, almost domesticated animals). Jesus, the Last Adam, had to conquer in the context of the chaos the first Adam's sin had brought into the world.

So from the beginning of his ministry to its end, Jesus is marching against the powers of darkness. Virtually immediately after the temptations, as he begins his public ministry, he has to face a further onslaught of demonic activity in the Nazareth synagogue.[44] Soon afterwards he encounters a man in Gadara whose life is under some destructive alien influence and out of control. He roams through the tombs like a wild animal nobody can subdue.

Jesus says tenderly to the demoniac, "What is your name?"

He replies, "My name is Legion, for we are many."[45]

---

[43] J. H. Newman, "Praise to the Holiest in the Height," from the poem *The Dream of Gerontius*, written in 1865 and later set to music by Edward Elgar for his oratorio of the same name.
[44] Luke 4:16–30.
[45] Mark 5:9.

A Roman legion theoretically consisted of around four thousand to five thousand soldiers. The man is saying, "Thousands of demons have invaded my life."

But catch this. It takes only one demon to destroy a man. Why, then, have thousands of demons invaded him? Because the Lord Jesus was there. That is the whole point. This is not simply a poor man possessed by a legion of demons. That would be an extravagant deployment of forces Satan could never afford. No, not this man, but the destruction of Jesus' ministry is the ultimate target.

The reason there is so much demon possession in the time period recorded by the Gospels is not—as is sometimes assumed—that demon possession was commonplace then. In fact it was not. Rather, the land then was demon-invaded because the Savior was marching to the victory promised in Genesis 3:15. And all hell was let loose in order to withstand him.

The response of the demons themselves to Jesus makes this clear. When he was confronted by the demon-possessed man in the Capernaum synagogue, the unclean spirit's reaction to him was "Have you come to destroy us?"[46]

And then, of course, this sinister opposition took a more subtle form in one of the three men Jesus loved most in the world, when Simon Peter echoed the Serpent's temptation of the Savior: "Don't take the way of the cross, Jesus."[47]

How resolute Jesus was—how clear-headed to hear in Peter's words the accent of the Evil One—and to respond: "Get behind me, Satan!"[48]

A Change of Tactic

In the first half of the Gospel narrative, up to the point where Peter confesses that Jesus is the Christ, Satan seeks to divert him

---

[46] Mark 1:24; cf. Matt. 8:29, "Have you come to torment us *before the time?*"
[47] See Matt. 16:22–23.
[48] Matt. 16:23; Mark 8:33.

from the cross. In the wilderness he says, "Jesus, don't go to the cross. I will give you the kingdoms as long as you will bow down and worship me." Through Simon Peter he says, "Don't go to the cross. Find some other way." The demons seem to say, "Don't go to the cross."

Then something unexpected happens. Satan's strategy moves into a different gear. Now he tries to get Jesus to the cross as quickly as he possibly can. Now he is attempting to subvert God's timing so that Jesus' death will be a terrible tragedy, not an obedient saving ministry. Now, instead of using an unstable member of the disciple band (Simon Peter), he uses its trusted treasurer (Judas Iscariot). Indeed his fellow disciples trusted him so implicitly that when he left the upper room to betray Jesus, several of them consciously thought that he was going to engage in mercy ministry.[49]

Satan had used Simon Peter—unsuccessfully. But now he actually came to indwell Judas Iscariot.[50] That signaled the beginning of Jesus' final conflict. "This" he said to his captors in the garden of Gethsemane, "is [your] hour, and the power of darkness."[51] That power would crush his heel. But in that conflict he would crush the head of the Serpent.

So the whole-Bible story is one of ongoing conflict. The Gospel story brings us to its crisis point.

Victory

How does Jesus crush the head of the Serpent and destroy his influence?

Where Adam conceded victory to Satan, Jesus resisted him. Total obedience to his Father marked the whole course of his life.

Three years later, Jesus was also brought to a tree. He too faced temptation. But in his case the temptation was to *not* eat of its poi-

---

[49] John 13:29.
[50] John 13:27.
[51] Luke 22:53.

sonous fruit. The obedient Last Adam reversed the disobedience of the first Adam.

God gave Adam and Eve the pleasure of eating fruit from every tree in the garden, except one. The forbidden fruit, as we have seen, was not an ugly fruit that looked sinister and gave off a repulsive odor. No, it looked delicious. Every instinct said, with respect to that tree, "This tree—like all the trees in the garden—is attractive to the eyes. Its fruit looks and smells delicious."[52]

Why, when the tree in Eden looked so attractive, had God said, "Do not eat this fruit"? The tree tested Adam's obedience. But it also provided a context in which he could grow in his relationship to God. For God was really saying to him: "Adam, obey me in this to show you trust and love me. By doing so you will grow in your relationship with me." Alas, Adam followed in the pathway on which his wife's senses had led her: sight, smell, and taste rather than the word of God.

When the second Man was brought to the Calvary tree, he faced a reversed mirror image of the first man's temptation.

There was nothing in the first tree that led Adam instinctively to resist the temptation to eat its delicious-looking fruit. So there was nothing in the second tree that attracted Jesus to eat its repulsive fruit of God-forsakenness. It was an accursed tree.[53]

There was not a bone in Christ's body, not an ounce of his flesh, not an affection in his soul that could ever be instinctively willing to experience a sense of abandonment by God. Everything in him shrunk from that. He loved his Father!

We can say more. Any other reaction than to shrink from death on the tree as repulsive would have been less than holy on Jesus' part. Jesus was called to experience something from which every instinct in him recoiled. Jesus had to NOT *want to eat* the fruit of the tree with his whole being, and yet be *willing to eat*. He willed

---

[52] See Gen. 2:9.
[53] See Gal. 3:13.

to be obedient when he did not want to be forsaken! Such was the price of our salvation. No wonder Jesus prayed, "Abba, Father. . . . Remove this cup from me."[54]

We can tabulate the contrast between Adam and Jesus in this way:

Two persons:	Adam the first	Adam the last
Two places:	The forbidden tree	The accursed tree
Two commands:	Do not eat the fruit!	Drink what is in the cup!
Two desires:	Wants to eat	Does not want to drink
Two actions:	Disobedience	Obedience
Two results:	Death	Life

It is against this background that Paul says, "He . . . [became] obedient to the point of death, even death on a cross."[55] Jesus willed to take the divine curse although everything in him, every holy desire, longed for and deserved the divine blessing. He took our place—who can fathom the mystery of his sense of desolation and alienation from heaven's glory? He bore the curse—all for love's sake.

> In my place, condemned he stood
> Sealed my pardon with his blood
> Hallelujah! What a Savior![56]

But there is more. Jesus did something else of massive importance.

The Unmasking

Jesus unmasked Satan's lie.

Paul describes the fall of man in these terms: "They exchanged

---

[54] Mark 14:36.
[55] Phil. 2:8.
[56] Philip Bliss, "Man of Sorrows," 1875.

the truth about God for a lie."[57] What was this lie? This, surely: the Serpent said to Eve:

> Your God has set you in this garden. He has given you so many rich and attractive trees, so much luscious fruit. But he is really saying: "I am surrounding you with all these beautiful and delicious things *BUT you are not to have any of them*."[58]

Do you see the satanic innuendo here? "God is cynical; he does not want the best for you, nor does he give the best to you. He is toying with you for his own malicious pleasure. He doesn't really love you. He despises you."

The rest is history. Eve struggled with the temptation, but the poisonous thought was already injected through her now-confused mind into her affections and will. From there it has passed down into our bloodstream. It is in our system now. It is the twist within us that leads us not to believe and not to trust that God himself and everything—absolutely everything—he is, does, says, commands, and promises is good.

Sometimes non-Christians say to us, "The God I believe in is a God of love." But they do not know themselves. For the Bible's analysis is: "No—you have exchanged the truth about God for a lie. You don't believe that he is love. You wouldn't live the way you do if you really believed that."

The heart of the gospel is: in demonstration of his love, the heavenly Father sent his only Son to die on the cross in our place and for our sins. "God demonstrated his love toward us, in that, while we were yet sinners, Christ died for us."[59]

It is the cross alone that ultimately proves the love of God to us—not the providential circumstances of our lives. We must not

---

[57] Rom. 1:25.
[58] See Gen. 3:1ff.
[59] Rom. 5:8.

allow ourselves to be tricked into thinking that *if* things are going well with us, then we can be sure of God's love. For life can often seem dark and painful. Things do not always go well for us. Rather, we look to the sacrifice of the cross and the demonstration God gave there of his love. This is the proof I need. This is the truth I need to hear if the lie is to be dispelled.

If Jesus has died for me, then I can be sure that the Father, the Son, and the Holy Spirit will stop at nothing (absolutely nothing!) to do me good:

> He who did not spare his own Son but gave him up for us all, how will he not also with him graciously give us all things?[60]

Notice how Calvary-oriented, cross-focused, and Christ-centered the gospel is. But Calvary, with all its dark sense of abandonment, is an even fuller revelation of grace. For it is not only

> 1) The high point of Jesus' obedience. He became "obedient to the point of death, even death on a cross."[61]

It is also:

> 2) The high point of the Father's love for his incarnate Son. "For this reason the Father loves me," Jesus said, "because I lay down my life."[62] The moment he cried out, "My God, I am forsaken! Why?" was the very moment that his Father, through his tears, was singing,

> My Jesus, I love thee,
> I know thou art mine . . .
> If ever I loved thee,
> My Jesus, 'tis now.

---

[60] Rom. 8:32.
[61] Phil. 2:8.
[62] John 10:17.

All of this took place in order to crush the Serpent's head and to squeeze from his fangs the poisonous lie that still deadens many a Christian's heart, and causes us to become fearful, doubting believers.

There is one further note to add that seems to shed light on Christ's work as the seed.

The Gardener Returns

Recall what Adam was created to be: the gardener.

Everything God made was "good"—but everything was not yet garden. God wanted Adam to exercise his dominion by expanding the garden. Having given him a garden to begin with, God was saying: "Now, Adam, I have given you a start." Just as we might say to our children, "Here is a start. Now you go and do the rest."

Adam was to "garden" the whole earth, for the glory of the heavenly Father. But he failed. Created to make the dust fruitful, he himself became part of the dust.[63] The garden of Eden became the wilderness of this world. But do you also remember how John's Gospel records what happened on the morning of Jesus' resurrection? He was "the beginning [of the new creation], the firstborn from the dead."[64] But Mary Magdalene did not recognize him; instead she spoke to him "supposing him to be the gardener."[65] Well, who else would he be, at that time in the morning?

The gardener? Yes, indeed. He is the Gardener. He is the second Man, the last Adam, who is now beginning to restore the garden.

Later that day Jesus showed his disciples where the nails and the spear had drawn blood from his hands and side. The Serpent had indeed crushed his heel. But he had crushed the Serpent's head! Now he was planning to turn the wilderness back into a garden. Soon he would send his disciples into the world with the good news

---

[63] Gen. 3:19.
[64] Col. 1:18.
[65] John 20:15.

of his victory. All authority on earth—lost by Adam—was now regained. The world must now be reclaimed for Jesus the conqueror!

In the closing scenes of the book of Revelation, John saw the new earth coming down from heaven. What did it look like? A garden in which the tree of life stands![66]

One day all of this will come to pass.

So the Seed has come; his heel oozed blood from being crushed. But the Serpent's head has been crushed in the process. Jesus reigns, and we will be more than conquerors through him who loved us![67]

But there is still a long way to go before the end; and there is much more to learn about Christ if we are to know him fully. Already we have had hints of what he will need to be: someone who speaks the truth that counters Satan's lies, that is, a prophet; someone who is able to assure us that our sins are forgiven, that is, a priest; and someone who is able to subdue us and reign over us, that is, a king. And much else.

---

[66] See Revelation 21–22.
[67] Rom. 8:37.

2

Jesus Christ,
the True Prophet

Scripture urges us to fix our eyes upon Jesus.[1]

Very few books have made more impact on our lives than the *Memoir and Remains of Robert Murray M'Cheyne*. Robert M'Cheyne was the Scottish minister of St. Peter's Church, Dundee, from 1836 to1843. He died at the age of twenty-nine. But his life, his preaching, and indeed his whole ministry were marked by a profound Christ-centeredness. We often reflect on his words: "Learn much of the Lord Jesus. For every look at yourself, take ten looks at Christ. Let your soul be filled with a sense of the excellence of Christ."[2]

This is our great need—to have our minds and hearts filled with a sense of the greatness and incomparable glory of Christ. When you think about the deeply narcissistic age in which we live and how much we are tempted and encouraged to be focused on ourselves, M'Cheyne's words still echo in our ears down through the corridors of time. We need to take them to heart every single day.

We have already noted that one of the "looks" we can take at Jesus is to see him as the seed of the woman. In addition to this, the Bible helps us to see him as the Christ. *Christ* means "anointed one." In the old covenant, three particular people were anointed for

---

[1] Heb. 12:1–2.
[2] Andrew Bonar, *Memoir and Remains of Robert Murray M'Cheyne* (1844; repr. Edinburgh: Banner of Truth, 1966), 293.

the service of God: the prophet, the priest, and the king. These three dimensions reveal more fully both his person and his work.

In many ways the church as a whole is indebted to John Calvin for explaining the importance of this "threefold office."

When Calvin introduced this theme in his *Institutes of the Christian Religion*, he noted that some of his contemporaries used these terms of Jesus "coldly and ineffectually, because they do not know what each of these truths contains."[3] Simply put, it is possible to be adept at using this phraseology, even in an erudite way, but yet leave hearts cold so that our teaching fails to express the power of the truth we are describing. We end up explaining concepts instead of pointing to Jesus himself. It is important, then, if we are going to employ this grid to help us understand Christ, that we use it properly.

In this chapter we will look at Jesus as the heaven-sent prophet and think of him in four ways.

The fundamentals of education used to be referred to as the "three R's"—reading, writing, and arithmetic. These are basic and essential to our ability to function in the world. In a similar way we might say there are four R's that are basic and essential to our knowing Christ as our prophet and enjoying communion with him.

R 1: Required

Our fallen condition *requires* us to have Jesus as our prophet. "Required" here is used in its most basic sense: "needed for a particular purpose; upon which we depend for success or survival."

Each of these three titles of Jesus—prophet, priest, king—contains an inherent judgment upon us. As king, Jesus comes to us to subdue our rebellion. As priest, he comes in order to deal with our sins. But the reason he comes to us as prophet is to deal with our ignorance.

Spiritual ignorance is the reason God sent prophets throughout

---

[3] John Calvin, *Institutes of the Christian Religion*, ed. J. T. McNeil, trans. Ford Lewis Battles (Philadelphia: Westminster, 1960), 2.15.1.

all biblical history—and ultimately sent his true and final prophet, the Lord Jesus.

Following the first sin and fall in Genesis 3, God saw that "every intention of the thoughts of his heart was only evil continually."[4] Man's heart and mind are now skewed in the wrong direction.

As we read on through the Bible, we discover something else: because of our willful rebellion, folly lurks in our hearts and further impacts our ignorance: "The fool says in his heart," says the psalmist, "there is no God."[5] By the time we reach into the New Testament, for example in Romans and then again in Ephesians, Paul is driving home the same truth:

> They became futile in their thinking, and their foolish hearts were darkened.[6]

> They are darkened in their understanding, alienated from the life of God because of the ignorance that is in them, due to their hardness of heart.[7]

Into this tragic situation of moral and spiritual ignorance Christ came. Through his prophetic ministry, light was to shine light into our darkness. "In him was life, and the life was the light of men."[8]

Children are naturally scared in the dark. That is why they ask, "Will you leave the light on in my bedroom?" Thomas Watson, the English Puritan, makes an insightful comment in this respect. He notes that while we see the dangers in natural darkness, in spiritual darkness we seem to know no fear.

> But the spiritual darkness is not accompanied with horror, men tremble not at their condition; nay, they like their condition well enough.[9]

---

[4] Gen. 6:5.
[5] Pss. 14:1; 53:1.
[6] Rom. 1:21.
[7] Eph. 4:18.
[8] John 1:4.
[9] Thomas Watson, *A Body of Divinity* (1692; repr. Edinburgh: Banner of Truth, 1958), 169.

Of course this is simply illustrating and reinforcing what John tells us. "People loved the darkness rather than the light because their works were evil."[10] In fact, this darkness—an internal darkness—is so deep that man, as man, is blind to the very fact of his blindness! He becomes conscious of it only when the Lord Jesus comes to reveal it to him. Because of his sin and his fallen condition, it is only by God's grace that he discovers eventually that there is no intellectual road to God. As Martin Luther observed, man by his very nature is *incurvatus in se*—turned in upon himself. As a result, his view of the world is not neutral; it is skewed. He is biased—about everything. "The heart of man," says John Calvin, "is a perpetual factory of idols."[11] Or, to quote William Temple, "every day in a thousand ways I make myself the center of the universe."[12]

Into that darkness and folly God has spoken through the prophets "in many and various ways."[13] The prophets speak with great clarity on this theme. They consistently say: "This is what the Lord says," and, "Listen to me, O House of Jacob. Listen to me, O House of Israel." The people must listen to the word of the Lord. "Old Testament prophecy was a means by which an infallible God used fallible men to bring an infallible word to fallible people."[14] The prophets confronted their contemporaries with the absolute folly and futility of idolatry.

Here is Isaiah at his most scathing:

> He cuts down cedars, or he chooses a cypress tree or an oak and lets it grow strong among the trees of the forest. He plants a cedar and the rain nourishes it. Then it becomes fuel for a man. He takes a part of it and warms himself; he kindles a fire and bakes bread. Also he makes a god and worships it; he makes it an idol and falls down before it. Half of it he burns in the fire.

---

[10] John 3:19.
[11] Calvin, *Institutes*, 1.11.8.
[12] Cited in James Philip, *The Growing Christian* (Ross-shire, UK: Christian Focus, 2010), 57.
[13] Heb. 1:1.
[14] John Blanchard, *Major Points from the Minor Prophets* (Carlisle, PA: Evangelical Press, 2012), 25.

Over the half he eats meat; he roasts it and is satisfied. Also he warms himself and says, "Aha, I am warm, I have seen the fire!" And the rest of it he makes into a god, his idol, and falls down to it and worships it. He prays to it and says, "Deliver me, for you are my god!"

They know not, nor do they discern, for he has shut their eyes, so that they cannot see, and their hearts, so that they cannot understand. No one considers, nor is there knowledge or discernment to say, "Half of it I burned in the fire; I also baked bread on its coals; I roasted meat and have eaten. And shall I make the rest of it an abomination? Shall I fall down before a block of wood?" He feeds on ashes; a deluded heart has led him astray, and he cannot deliver himself or say, "Is there not a lie in my right hand?"[15]

Now, when we read that, we are tempted to say to ourselves, "That was a long time ago, and we have moved beyond such folly." But the truth is, we continue to manufacture our own gods—invariably made in our own image. These gods of our own invention take many different forms but share a view of reality that is essentially pantheistic. "All of them, in one way or another, assume that nature encloses and contains the sacred. And it assumes that the way we make contact with God is to find Him in ourselves. He is there within our deepest self."[16]

A recent editorial in our local newspaper described the Christmas spirit as the celebration of belief in the existence of an eternal energy! Discovering this energy within, in a way that is profoundly personal, was seen in an extreme form in the 1980s book *Habits of the Heart*.[17] We are introduced to Sheila Larson, a young nurse who has invented her own religion in which God is defined as whatever fulfills her needs. She described this "faith" quite unashamedly as "Sheilaism."

---

[15] Isa. 44:14–20.

[16] David F. Wells, *What Is the Trinity?* Basics of the Faith (Philipsburg, NJ: P&R, 2012), 11.

[17] Robert N. Bellah and Richard Madsen, *Habits of the Heart: Individualism and Commitment in American Life* (Berkeley, CA: University of California Press, 1985).

G. K. Chesterton shrewdly commented on this kind of thinking when he said that once people stop believing in the God of the Bible, they don't believe in nothing—they begin to believe in anything!

This is why we need a prophet who is able to dethrone our ignorance. And unless we are delivered from it by this great and true prophet, we remain in the darkness and futility of our thinking.

R 2: Revealed

Our second word is—not surprisingly—"revealed." "Long ago, at many times and in many ways, God spoke to our fathers by the prophets, but in these last days," says the writer to the Hebrews, "he has spoken to us by his Son."[18]

This prophetic, revelatory role is a vital part of the ministry of Jesus.

While Moses was the first major prophet, he spoke of another prophet who was to come: "The LORD your God will raise up for you a prophet like me from among you, from your brothers—it is to him you shall listen." And again, "The LORD said to me, 'They are right in what they have spoken. What they say is good. I will raise up for them a prophet like you from among their brothers. And I will put my words in his mouth, and he shall speak to them all that I command him.' "[19]

This is a perfect description of our Lord's prophetic ministry: God puts his words into Jesus' mouth. Jesus reveals everything his Father has commanded him. These words also surely lie behind our Lord's High Priestly Prayer in John 17. It is the prayer of the Great Prophet:

> Now they know that everything that you have given me is from you. For I have given them the words that you gave me, and they

---

[18] Heb. 1:1–2.
[19] Deut. 18:15–18.

have received them and have come to know in truth that I came from you; and they have believed that you sent me.[20]

An expectation of this ministry of Christ runs throughout the Old Testament into the New. Calvin comments that the minds of the pious [have] always been imbued with the conviction that they were to hope for the full light of understanding only at the coming of the Messiah."[21] Think, for example, of the way the aged Simeon took the baby Jesus in his arms in the temple. What does he say? "My eyes have seen your salvation . . . a light for revelation to the Gentiles," and so on.[22] In the deep piety of his expectation, he was looking for the embodiment and the fulfillment of the ancient prophetic word.

We see the same thing illustrated in Jesus' conversation with the unnamed Samaritan woman he met at Jacob's well. Such an expectation (as Calvin also notes) "had spread even beyond the realms of the faithful, and had infiltrated the minds of the Samaritans."[23] She knew enough theology to be able to say to Jesus, "When [the Messiah comes], he will tell us all things."[24] What a fascinating statement from an unlikely source! Here is a Samaritan woman who has already had multiple husbands and now has a live-in lover. She meets this Jewish stranger at the well, and an unexpected conversation begins. It is really remarkable, isn't it? As Jesus speaks to her, she immediately responds, "I can see that you are a prophet." And then as the dialogue continues, she seeks, as it were, to put an end to it all by simply telling this stranger this whole thing will get sorted out when the Messiah comes. "Because when he comes—all of this will become absolutely clear." Little did she expect Jesus' response: "I who speak to you am he."[25] Her amazement is matched by that of the congregation in the synagogue of Nazareth when

---

[20] John 17:7–8.
[21] Calvin, *Institutes*, 2.15.1.
[22] Luke 2:30–32.
[23] Calvin, *Institutes*, 2.15.1.
[24] John 4:25.
[25] John 4:26.

Jesus, having read from Isaiah 61, declares, "Today this Scripture has been fulfilled in your hearing."[26] They marveled at his words!

It was *as a prophet* that Jesus was first acclaimed by his contemporaries. We see this throughout the Gospels. Immediately following the feeding of the five thousand, the word on everyone's lips is: "This indeed is *the Prophet* who is to come into the world!"[27]

When Jesus stopped a funeral procession outside the city of Nain, it was to raise the dead boy and restore him to his mother. In response the people say, "A *great prophet* has arisen among us."[28]

When Nicodemus, the profoundly learned and deeply religious Pharisee, came to Jesus under cover of darkness with some questions, he said: "You know, I can see that you are a teacher sent from God." In other words, "I can see that you are *a prophet*."[29] And later when Jesus asked his disciples, "What is the word on the street concerning me? Who do people say that I am?" one of the first responses is "Many say that you are *one of the prophets*."[30]

Jesus accepted this designation—although he wanted it to be properly understood, because it wasn't. For example, after the evening in the synagogue in Nazareth, he sensed the hostile reaction of the people and declared: "No *prophet* is acceptable in his hometown."[31]

Later on he says that it is not right for a prophet to die outside of Jerusalem.[32]

We need a prophet because of our ignorance. Jesus himself is a prophet; indeed he is *the* prophet we need.

R 3: Recognized

This takes us a stage further than "revealed." Ultimately Jesus must be recognized, not merely as a messenger of revelation from

---

[26] Luke 4:21.
[27] John 6:14.
[28] Luke 7:16.
[29] See John 3:1–2.
[30] See Matt. 16:14.
[31] Luke 4:24.
[32] Luke 13:33.

God but as the very source of that revelation. Jesus is not only the revealer; he *is* the revelation! That is why after his words in the Nazareth synagogue the buzz around town was: "Isn't this Joseph's son? Who does he think he is, reading the Scriptures in such a way? Who does he think he is, adopting the position of a teacher? Who, then, is this man on whom our eyes were fixed like magnets? Who is this who says, 'Today this Scripture is fulfilled in your hearing'?"[33]

And then, as we saw in the first chapter, the same thing happens again on the road to Emmaus. The discouraged disciples had no idea that they were speaking to the one who had risen from the dead. And so, as they engage in conversation, he gently rebukes them:

> "O foolish ones, and slow of heart to believe all that the prophets have spoken! Was it not necessary that the Christ should suffer these things and enter into his glory?" And beginning with Moses and all the Prophets, he interpreted to them in all the Scriptures the things concerning himself.[34]

Now, none of the other prophets could say that, could they? Jesus is the embodiment of all that the prophets have previously said. Essentially, Jesus is able to take the Scriptures as they are, open them up, and say: "Do you see? This is a book about me. This whole book is about me!"

As Jesus explained the Scriptures to them, their eyes were opened. They heard a careful exposition of the Scriptures; they experienced the illumination of their minds, and they discovered a new passion stirring in their hearts—a fire. Then they *recognized* him!

> And their eyes were opened, and they recognized him. And he vanished from their sight. They said to each other, "Did not our

---

[33] See Luke 4:16–22.
[34] Luke 24:25–27.

hearts burn within us while he talked to us on the road, while he opened to us the Scriptures?"[35]

Jesus did the same in his subsequent appearance to the disciples. Not only did he come to open the Scriptures, and to open hearts, but now "he opened their minds to understand the Scriptures, and said to them, 'Thus it is written, that the Christ should suffer and . . . rise from the dead.'"[36] "This is what was written then," Jesus said, "and now what has happened in me is the fulfillment of it all." This was all part of his plan to prepare these same disciples to go out in the power of the Spirit of God to preach the truth embodied in him as God's final prophet.[37]

The prophetic role of Jesus is *required* in order to dispel our ignorance. It is *revealed* in Jesus himself. It is *recognized* in all of its fullness at the end of his earthly ministry.

But there is one further step we need to take if we are fully to capture what it means for Jesus to be prophet. These first three aspects describe his *finished* work, his fulfilled ministry. But there is a fourth aspect—his *unfinished* work. For the Lord Jesus continues to minister as God's prophet.

R 4: Realized

Jesus' ministry as prophet needs to be realized—but how? In the preaching and teaching of the Bible. Christ's prophetic ministry was continued in the preaching and teaching ministry of the apostles. But the same is also true of all preachers who stand in the line of that apostolic authority and have been set apart as gifts of the ascended Christ. It is their ongoing task to bring the Scriptures to bear upon the minds of the foolish and ignorant in their own time and generation.

---

[35] Luke 24:31–32.
[36] Luke 24:45.
[37] See Luke 24:46–49.

If we fail to understand this, then both our preaching and our hearing of the biblical testimony to Christ will be impoverished. Calvin, again, helps us here. He says of Jesus:

> He received anointing, not only for himself that he might carry out the office of teaching, but for his whole body that the power of the Spirit might be present in the continuing preaching of the gospel.[38]

So the present prophetic ministry of Christ never introduces bizarre or strange or new and fanciful notions. No, it is found in the opening up of the Word, in the gossiping of the gospel, in the sharing of Christ. That is where the ongoing prophetic work of Christ is seen—or, better, heard. That is what Paul is saying when he writes to the Corinthians: "Therefore, we are ambassadors for Christ, God making his appeal through us."[39] Through him? Through Timothy? Through Titus? Doesn't that also imply: through us? God is making his appeal through us!

At the close of his earthly ministry Jesus said to his disciples, "I want you to go out from here into the world and preach the gospel. But listen, I am always with you."

These men were going out to be confronted by a hostile world, deeply aware of their own finitude, personal frailty, and ineffectiveness. Jesus was giving them a cast-iron promise: "And I will be there. I was once lifted up on the cross and I will be lifted up again through your witness in order to draw all men to myself."[40]

The task of sharing the gospel involves simply and clearly bearing testimony to Christ. It involves saying who he is and what he has accomplished historically, explaining the significance of his death, the wonder of his resurrection, the fact of his ascension, and so on. And the promise of Christ is that in this ongoing ministry of

---

[38] Calvin, *Institutes*, 2.15.2.
[39] 2 Cor. 5:20.
[40] See John 12:32.

God's Word, he is present and he continues to speak. But there will need to be more said about that in a later chapter.[41]

Passion

There is a vast difference between simply conveying information to people, which can be cold and ineffectual, and true preaching and witness.

We have a long-standing friend who was once driving in the north of Scotland with our fellow countryman the late professor John Murray of Westminster Seminary in Philadelphia. Professor Murray decided to turn the journey into a quiz! He asked a question: "What is the difference between a lecture and preaching?"

Our friend tried his best to come up with a good answer. But Professor Murray was not satisfied.

"Well, Professor Murray," our friend eventually conceded, "What is the answer? What is the difference between a lecture and preaching?"

"This is what it is:" said John Murray, "Preaching is a personal, passionate plea."

Our friend again replied, "But *what* is the personal passionate plea?"

Quick as a flash, Professor Murray responded in Paul's words: "We implore you on behalf of Christ, be reconciled to God."[42]

That's it!

This is not just for the pulpit and the big public occasion. This is for the grocery store, for the golf course, for the coffee shop. Wherever we tell others about the Lord Jesus, through God's power and with an awareness that Christ himself is the great prophet of God, we say—in our own words—"I implore you. Be reconciled to God. Receive the reconciliation that he has provided." And when God begins to work, people say, "I didn't know about that; tell me

---

[41] See below, pp. 68–71.
[42] 2 Cor. 5:20.

more." And we can respond, "Well then, I will be glad to tell you about it. Let me tell you the story." And so we have the opportunity to speak into the darkness of their minds and the futility of their thinking.[43]

It is essential that we do this as humble instruments of the ongoing ministry of Christ. Listen to John Calvin again:

> All those, then, who, not content with the gospel, patch it with something extraneous to it, detract from Christ's authority.[44]

We must be alert to this danger! Why would he say, "from Christ's authority?" Because it is Christ's prophetic word—in the preaching and teaching of the Bible—that is brought to bear upon our minds through the very feebleness of the instruments God chooses to use.

There is enormous encouragement for us in that. If that were not the case, then we wouldn't really know who was doing what, would we? But when we're aware of the fact that he has put this treasure in "jars of clay,"[45] we say, "Well, it must be God who is doing this!" Listen to Calvin on this same theme:

> He deigns to consecrate the mouths and tongues of men to His service, making His own voice to be heard in them. And whenever God is pleased to bless their labour, He makes their doctrine efficacious by the power of His Spirit; and the voice which is in itself mortal, is made an instrument to communicate eternal life.[46]

James S. Stewart, in the Lyman Beecher lectures delivered at Yale, uses a wonderful expression. He describes the apostles hitting the streets of Jerusalem "with a waft of the supernatural."[47]

---

[43] Rom. 1:21.

[44] Calvin, *Institutes*, 2.15.2.

[45] 2 Cor. 4:7.

[46] Cited in James Philip, *Pulpit and People*, ed. M. Cameron and S. Ferguson (Edinburgh: Rutherford House, 1986), 13.

[47] James S. Stewart, *A Faith to Proclaim: The Lyman Beecher Lectures at Yale University* (London: Hodder & Stoughton, 1966), 45.

With a waft of the supernatural! He is not thinking about some of the strange and eccentric things we see on religious television. He is talking about what Peter must have felt on the Day of Pentecost.

Knowing how close he had been to becoming a complete wash-out, on the Day of Pentecost Peter finds himself surrounded by his fellow countrymen plus visitors from abroad. There he stands—in the very same streets of Jerusalem where he'd run to hide a few weeks before as someone who had denied he even knew Jesus. But now he addresses the crowd with such boldness and with a clarity of understanding of the Bible's message that is simply breathtaking. That day three thousand people were baptized! Oh, yes, there was "a waft of the supernatural," all right.

Isn't there supposed to be?

To quote Donald McCullough: "When the gospel is preached, . . . Christ walks among his people. It's the miracle of Christmas all over again: Christ clothed himself in humanity, spurning the language of angels to speak with the tongues of mortals."[48]

Two further things need to be said here by way of application.

Bold Confidence

If we accept this, if we bow down before the truth of Christ's prophetic ministry and then stand up on our feet ready to serve the Lord, something will happen. We will be endued with a sense of confidence, a God-emboldened confidence, and the kind of confidence that will allow us to be courageous in the face of all the challenges of our day. It will make us bold enough—not bombastic, but bold enough—to be faithful to our Lord and his commission despite all the pluralism and syncretism of our culture.

This will give us the courage to say that there is no other name under heaven among men by which people can be saved.[49] We will

---

[48] Donald McCullough, *The Trivialization of God: The Dangerous Illusion of a Manageable Deity* (Colorado Springs, CO: NavPress, 1995), 127.
[49] Acts 4:12.

not be embarrassed that Jesus said, "I am the way, and the truth, and the life . . . ," nor will we put a full stop there but be prepared to go on to finish Jesus' statement: ". . . No one comes to the Father except through me."[50] We will be unashamed of the exclusivism of Christ's salvation—he alone is the way to God and the only mediator between man and God. And we will be encouraged to tell others about him because we know that "he is able to save to the uttermost those who draw near to God through him."[51]

There is a gracious boldness that comes from this.

In the sixteenth century John Knox encouraged Scottish ministers by reminding them that when the prophetic Word was heard in the exposition of Scripture, "wayfaring men, though fools, would meet their God in the Bible, hear His voice, take His promises and comforts and rebukes personally and directly to themselves, and understand enough of what was being said to them to receive, by faith, salvation."[52]

Genuine Compassion

But alongside this boldness there is another result of the conviction that Christ is our true prophet: *compassion*—a compassion that leads us in the words of the old hymn:

> Rescue the perishing, care for the dying,
> Snatch them in pity from sin and the grave;
> Weep o'er the erring one, lift up the fallen,
> Tell them of Jesus, the mighty to save.[53]

Some of us are good at boldness but not so good at compassion. We gravitate to all the bold verses but turn away from the gospel's call to show genuine empathy.

---

[50] John 14:6.
[51] Heb. 7:25.
[52] Cited in Philip, *Pulpit and People*, 12.
[53] Fanny Crosby, "Rescue the Perishing," 1869.

We need to remember the boldness of Jesus. He is the Christ whose zeal for his Father's house consumed him in the temple. He is the Christ who drove out the moneychangers because they were turning his Father's house into a supermarket.[54] And he is the Christ who set his face steadfastly to go to Jerusalem and the cross—always about his Father's business.

But we must never lose sight of the fact that when Jesus, having sung with other pilgrims the songs of ascent,[55] arrived in Jerusalem, he cried out,

> O Jerusalem, Jerusalem, the city that kills the prophets and stones those who are sent to it! How often would I have gathered your children together as a hen gathers her brood under her wings, and you were not willing.[56]

When we recognize Jesus as the true prophet, exercising his ministry with compassionate boldness, then we may learn, despite our natural weakness to be bold with a boldness that comes from him. And despite our natural selfishness, to discover a compassion that comes from Christ and makes us say: "Oh, Cleveland, Cleveland! Oh, Columbia, Columbia! Oh, Glasgow, Glasgow!"—or wherever you happen to live.

As Christ's ministry now begins to unfold, we see that the designation "prophet" is inadequate to fully express the wonder of all he is and does. That is why we should never think of him as prophet except in the context of his *threefold office*. His prophetic ministry must never be isolated from his other two offices, as if somehow or another we could view Christ as prophet apart from his also being priest and king. Newton keeps them together in his hymn, "How Sweet the Name of Jesus Sounds":

---

[54] John 2:13–17.
[55] Psalms 120–134.
[56] Matt. 23:37–39.

Jesus, my shepherd, husband, friend
My prophet, priest and king
My Lord, my life, my way, my end
Accept the praise I bring.

We must then move on to consider Christ as priest and king.

3

Jesus Christ,
the Great High Priest

Sometimes—especially in the United States—people will uninten-tionally invade our private space just a little by asking, "Do you have a life verse?" We understand what they mean: "Is there a text in Scripture that has been a guide to you throughout the whole of your Christian life?"

Some people seem so bold in asking us this question that in whimsical moments we imagine them breaking through the crowds going straight up to the apostle Paul and asking, "So, Paul, do you have a life verse?"

Would he say, do you think, "Haven't you read my letters?"

Perhaps the verse that comes nearest to Paul's "life verse" is Philippians 3:8:

> I count everything as loss because of the surpassing worth of knowing Christ Jesus my Lord.

In simple terms he says, "I want to know Christ."

That was not merely a personal testimony, for Paul assumes this should be the life testimony of every Christian. He goes on to say:

> Every one of you who thinks about himself as a mature Christian should think this way. And if you think otherwise, then God will lead you back to this by his grace.[1]

---

[1] See Phil. 3:15.

This is the conviction that drives each of these chapters. So, having seen what is involved in Christ being prophet, we now turn to reflect on what it means to have him as our priest.

"Priest" is the only title given to Jesus that has virtually an entire book of the New Testament devoted to explaining it—the letter to the Hebrews.

Hebrews is an anonymous letter. Its author describes it as a brief word of encouragement or exhortation.[2] Central to this encouragement is his exhortation to "Consider Jesus,"[3] to be "looking to Jesus"[4]—and especially to see him as our high priest.

Facing Trials

Why was that important to these Hebrews?

They had experienced the same trials as Paul did when he became a Christian.

First, they would have been disinherited. They "suffered the loss of all things."[5] That must have been the fate of many Jews who had come to faith in Jesus as the Messiah. Still today when a member of a strict orthodox Jewish family becomes a Christian, he or she may be literally disinherited.

So, clearly, many of these young Christians had suffered great material privation as the result of their faith in Christ.[6] Not only were they personally *disinherited*, but they were both socially and spiritually *excommunicated*.

Put yourself in their shoes. You are a solid, law-abiding citizen of Memphis, or Columbia, or Cleveland, or Edinburgh, or London—or wherever. But because of your commitment to Jesus Christ, you are disinherited. What automatically follows? You become *persona non grata* in all the societies, clubs, networks, and

---

[2] Heb. 13:22.
[3] Heb. 3:1.
[4] Heb. 12:2.
[5] Phil. 3:8.
[6] Heb. 10:32–34.

social friendships (and children's schools!) that have made up the fabric of your life. All that is now closed to you. You are excommunicated from family and society.

In addition there is the place of worship you attended from childhood. Its people, services, ceremonies, songs, liturgy, and all its activities were deeply ingrained in your life. Only now, when you are no longer there, do you realize the extent to which these things defined your identity. But now you are no longer welcome there. That church—still standing there as a reminder of the community that reared you and the identity you once had as part of it—is one you are no longer a part of. Instead you now meet with a number of others in the sitting room of a friend. All the things you used to enjoy—once so "meaningful" to you—rituals, officiating ministers, liturgies, music, worship ensembles, large crowds, special days of celebration—they are all gone. Now you meet in someone's house, and they don't even have a piano!

That was the situation of the first readers of Hebrews. No longer was their worship marked by the grandeur of the temple, the mass choir, the special moments. No longer did they catch sight of the high priest—the only man who, once a year, on the Day of Atonement, was allowed to enter the sacred room to seek God's forgiveness for the people. No longer do they wait for him to reappear and raise his hands in the historic words of the Aaronic blessing, assuring them of the Lord's benediction and his peace because "there is forgiveness with him." That visible sense that their sins had once again been covered and that the face of God was smiling upon them as his covenant people—it is all gone, never to return unless . . .

Tempted to Go Back

Unless what?

Unless they go back.

Some of them were tempted to go back.

Perhaps you are in a church that the whole congregation loves deeply, where the worship is God-centered, the preaching biblical, the fellowship caring, the vision for world missions strong, and the spiritual needs of the flock met. You have had dear friends whose company moved them to another location. They look for a new church home. But whenever you speak on the phone with them and ask how they are doing, they say, "Fine, except . . . oh, if only we could be back again in our old church; we just can't find anything like it here!"

That was the situation for the first readers of Hebrews. In former days they could see and touch and even smell the worship services—the great company of people, the music, all of the glorious aspects of Old Testament worship that God had given. Now it was all gone.

Was it all gone—for nothing?

What was the answer? How could the author of Hebrews write anything to encourage them in this situation? His response is to say:

> Don't turn back. If you are tempted to it, then you have been looking in the wrong direction. You have been seeing things from the wrong perspective! You are not looking far enough! You're not seeing clearly enough! Don't you see what is really important? Get your eyes off buildings and liturgies and crowds and music. Fix your eyes on Jesus!

Listen to some of the things he says about Jesus to encourage them:

1) They have a great high priest:

> Since then we have a great high priest who has passed through the heavens, Jesus, the Son of God, let us hold fast our confession. For we do not have a high priest who is unable to sympathize with our weaknesses, but one who in every respect has been tempted as we are, yet without sin. Let us then with confidence

draw near to the throne of grace, that we may receive mercy and find grace to help in time of need.[7]

2) They have a real salvation:

The former priests were many in number, because they were prevented by death from continuing in office, but he holds his priesthood permanently, because he continues forever. Consequently, he is able to save to the uttermost those who draw near to God through him, since he always lives to make intercession for them.[8]

3) They have a perfect high priest:

For it was indeed fitting that we should have such a high priest, holy, innocent, unstained, separated from sinners, and exalted above the heavens. He has no need, like those high priests, to offer sacrifices daily, first for his own sins and then for those of the people, since he did this once for all when he offered up himself.[9]

4) They have a better high priest:

They [the high priests of Israel] serve a copy and shadow of the heavenly things. . . . But as it is, Christ has obtained a ministry that is as much more excellent than the old as the covenant he mediates is better, since it is enacted on better promises.[10]

5) They have a final sacrifice:

But when Christ appeared as a high priest of the good things that have come, then through the greater and more perfect tent (not made with hands, that is, not of this creation) he entered once for all into the holy places, not by means of the blood of goats and calves but by means of his own blood, thus securing an eternal redemption.[11]

---

[7] Heb. 4:14–16.
[8] Heb. 7:23–25.
[9] Heb. 7:26–28.
[10] Heb. 8:5–6.
[11] Heb. 9:11–12.

6) They have a better sanctuary:

> For you have not come to what may be touched. . . . But you
> have come to Mount Zion and to the city of the living God, the
> heavenly Jerusalem, and to innumerable angels in festal gather-
> ing, and to the assembly of the firstborn who are enrolled in
> heaven, and to God, the judge of all, and to the spirits of the
> righteous made perfect, and to Jesus, the mediator of a new
> covenant, and to the sprinkled blood that speaks a better word
> than the blood of Abel.[12]

The author is really saying to them:

> What will keep you going in the way of the gospel of Jesus
> Christ is catching a glimpse of his greatness, and why it is he is
> such a *great* high priest. You have not lost—you have gained.
> You do not have less—you have more. Christ has done every-
> thing generations of high priests could not do. They were only
> shadows—he is the reality!

Two Dimensions

We saw that Jesus' ministry as prophet has both a finished and an
unfinished dimension. They are both present in each of Jesus' offices—prophetic, priestly, and kingly.

There is a *finished work of Christ*.

> All his work is ended,
> Joyfully we sing.
> Jesus has ascended,
> Glory to our King.[13]

He has cried, "It is finished."[14] In his death and resurrection he has
done everything necessary for our salvation to be accomplished.

---

[12] Heb. 12:18–24.
[13] Frances Ridley Havergal, "Golden Harps Are Sounding," 1871.
[14] John 19:30.

But then he applies it.

There is also, therefore, an *unfinished work of Christ.* Jesus has an ongoing ministry. As prophet he continues to speak to man from God.[15] Hebrews 2 brings these two dimensions together in a remarkable way. It describes Christ's finished work.

> Since therefore the children share in flesh and blood, he himself likewise partook of the same things, that through death he might destroy the one who has the power of death, that is, the devil, and deliver all those who through fear of death were subject to lifelong slavery. For surely it is not angels that he helps, but he helps the offspring of Abraham. Therefore he had to be made like his brothers in every respect, so that he might become a merciful and faithful high priest in the service of God, to make propitiation for the sins of the people.[16]

Notice the two aspects of Christ's work here:[17]

1) He delivers us from bondage to Satan:

> Since therefore the children share in flesh and blood, he himself likewise partook of the same things, that through death he might destroy the one who has the power of death, that is, the devil, and deliver all those who through fear of death were subject to lifelong slavery.[18]

2) He delivers us from the wrath of God:

> Therefore he had to be made like his brothers in every respect, so that he might become a merciful and faithful high priest in the service of God, to make propitiation for the sins of the people.[19]

---

[15] As we shall see, as King he continues to establish his kingdom and to rule over man for God.
[16] Heb. 2:14–17; John 19:30.
[17] See also Isa. 41:8–9; Luke 22:28; John 1:14; 16:11; Rom. 8:15; 15:17; 1 Cor. 15:54–56; Phil. 2:7; Col. 2:15; 2 Tim. 1:10; Heb. 2:14–18; 4:15–16; 5:1–2, 7–8; 8:9; 1 John 3:8.
[18] Heb. 2:14–15.
[19] Heb. 2:17.

He does both of these things through his ministry as priest. His sin offering of himself deals with our guilt and propitiates God's wrath and therefore sets us free from the grip of Satan. Since Christ has tasted death for us,[20] for believers death is no longer the wages of sin but has become the entrance into everlasting life. The leverage that Satan has used to fill us with fear has been destroyed. We are free at last.

Hebrews contrasts Christ's finished work with the never-ending work of the Old Testament priests as they brought animal sacrifices every day. But these could never take away sin because:

- They were repeated day by day. Since that was so, it is obvious that they could not fully and finally take away guilt.
- They were inadequate, even inappropriate, sacrifices for man's sin. How can an animal possibly substitute for the sins of a man or a woman?[21]

But Jesus offered *himself* as a sacrifice—man in place of men. His full, perfect, appropriate sacrifice was accepted by God. That is why God raised him from the dead. He is now seated at God's right hand. He does not continue to stand like the priest of old, in a daily repetition of his sacrifice. He has no need to! As the high priest who is himself the sacrifice, he has finished his atoning work.

In Christ our sins are fully and finally forgiven![22]

The Day of Atonement

There is a remarkable picture of this in the Old Testament in the annual Day of Atonement.[23] On that day, the high priest would take two goats. One of them would be slain and its blood offered as a sacrifice. But over the other he would confess the sins of the

---

[20] Heb. 2:9.
[21] Heb. 10:3.
[22] Heb. 9:12.
[23] Lev. 16:1–34.

people before it was taken out into the wilderness by the hand of a man who was ready to do it. This "scapegoat" carried into the wilderness the sins confessed over its head. It was then released into no-man's land, bearing the people's sin and guilt.

This presents a vivid illustration of the two aspects of Jesus' atoning work on the cross.

Jesus shed his own blood as the high priest who gave himself on the cross as the final sacrifice for our sins. But, on the cross, he was also taken, through the power of the Spirit, into the no-man's land between heaven and earth. In that lonely wilderness where he bore our sins, he experienced an indescribable sense of alienation from God. He was rejected by man and tasted death as the wages of our sin and as the curse of God.

Jesus went into the presence of God as if he were the only sinner in the world, enduring the wrath of God. Entering into the unspeakable black hole of desolation, he cried out, "My God, my God, why am I forsaken by you?" There, in the darkness, he became both the sacrifice and the scapegoat for our sins. His blood, shed for us, sets guilty consciences free and brings us peace with God.

> His blood can make the foulest clean
> His blood availed for me.[24]

Nothing Left to Fear

Would that every psychiatrist, every therapist, every personal counselor in the country understood that sin, guilt, the wrath of God, and therefore the fear of death create all other fears and lurk underneath all manner of neuroses. Until this central fear is dealt with, these other fears must linger on. Why is that? Because only when we are delivered from the great fear—the fear of death and judgment—will other fears become trivial. They can be dissolved

---

[24] Charles Wesley, "And Can It Be That I Should Gain?," 1738.

only by the knowledge that I need not fear death because the guilt of my sin has been borne by my Savior.

We have another friend in Scotland, a distinguished professor of mathematics. A number of years ago, one of his daughters, a young freshman Christian student, died suddenly. One moment from the day of her funeral has etched itself permanently into our memory. Our friend was borne along through the day by the grace of God. His quiet words as we greeted him were: "We know now that we have nothing left to fear."

That's it—nothing left to fear.

All this is true only because Jesus has dealt with our greatest problem.

That problem is not simply that of our fear. Our greatest problem is God himself. For by nature, we are under his wrath—and deserve to be. If we cannot deal with our sin and guilt, we certainly cannot deal with the wrath of God. But it was precisely to bear that wrath that the Lord Jesus, as our high priest, went into the holy place, the very presence of the holy God, and there experienced the awful unleashing of divine judgment.

This is why, when the resurrected Jesus revealed himself to his disciples, his first word was "*Shalom*! Peace! Now at last you may have peace with God."[25]

This is Christ's finished work as priest.

Most Christians are familiar with the *finished* work of Christ but less so with his *unfinished* work. But the author of Hebrews helps us to understand that although Jesus is "*seated* at the right hand of God," having finished his atoning work, he is still doing something. He now undertakes his *unfinished* work.

Unfinished Work

One thing you would probably learn if you spent time with us is that our Sunday school teachers taught us all kinds of hymns and

---

[25] Luke 24:36.

songs that we rarely hear today. One with which our class always began was this:

> Jesus, stand among us
> In Thy risen power.
> Let this time of worship
> Be a hallowed hour.[26]

What do we mean, "Jesus, *stand among us*"?

If you are not a Christian, you will have little or no idea what that is all about. It will be a total mystery. That may be one reason why, if you attend worship services, you find the Bible dull, hymns simply strange, and sermons boring. You have never experienced the presence of Jesus standing among his people, making the Bible a living book, the hymns making sense, and the sermons life-transforming.

A young man started attending services in a church where another of our friends is minister. After some time he came to living faith in Christ and applied for membership. The elders interviewed him. He told them how their church had changed dramatically since he first started attending. Now the music was so much better, the hymns chosen were much more singable than before, and—turning to the minister, he added, "Your sermons—well, I don't know what's happened to you, but they really connect now and make so much sense! You have really improved them!"

The elders were wise and mature men and probably smiled inwardly. They knew where the real change had taken place—in the young man himself. He had become a Christian. Now he was beginning to experience the difference it makes to know Christ present among his people.

The author of Hebrews teaches us that this is a central element in Jesus' ongoing priestly ministry. He is among his people when they come together. He is present in their worship.

---

[26] William Pennefather, "Jesus Stand among Us," 1855.

Hebrews 8:2 describes Jesus as a *leitourgos*. He is the high priest who is a minister in the holy places. You can probably see the English words *liturgy* and *liturgist* in that Greek word. The Greek word refers to the person who leads a service of worship. This is Jesus' ongoing ministry—he leads the worship of his people.

Worship Leader

Jesus leads every worship service you attend! He is the "worship leader."

You may be the music director in a church, or its organist, or sing in its choir, or play in its worship ensemble; you may even be its minister. But the one thing you are *not* is the worship leader. Jesus is the worship leader.

Earlier in Hebrews, the author gave some major hints about what this ministry of Jesus involves:

> For it was fitting that he, for whom and by whom all things exist, in bringing many sons to glory, should make the founder of their salvation perfect through suffering. For he who sanctifies and those who are sanctified all have one origin. That is why he is not ashamed to call them brothers, saying,

> > "I will tell of your name to my brothers;
> >   in the midst of the congregation I will sing your
> >   praise."

> And again,

> > "I will put my trust in him."

> And again,

> > "Behold, I and the children God has given me."[27]

---

27 Heb. 2:10–13.

Notice here how the words of Psalm 22:22 are put into Jesus' mouth. This is surely significant. It was to Psalm 22 that he turned during the latter hours of his crucifixion.[28] That psalm begins in overwhelming darkness: "My God, My God, why have you forsaken me?"[29] But it ends in words of triumph, which Hebrews applies to Jesus' resurrection, ascension, *and his ongoing* ministry—particularly aspects of his ongoing ministry that we often ignore:

> I will tell of your name to my brothers;
>> in the midst of the congregation I will praise you:
> You who fear the LORD, praise him!
>> All you offspring of Jacob, glorify him,
>> and stand in awe of him, all you offspring of Israel!
> For he has not despised or abhorred
>> the affliction of the afflicted,
> and he has not hidden his face from him,
>> but has heard, when he cried to him.
>
> From you comes my praise in the great congregation;
>> my vows I will perform before those who fear him.
> The afflicted shall eat and be satisfied;
>> those who seek him shall praise the LORD!
>> May your hearts live forever!
>
> All the ends of the earth shall remember
>> and turn to the LORD,
> and all the families of the nations
>> shall worship before you.
> For kingship belongs to the LORD,
>> and he rules over the nations.[30]

Jesus, the Preacher of the Word

Jesus is the worship leader, first, because he comes by his Spirit to minister his Word. He says, "I will tell of your name to my brothers."

---

[28] Matt. 27:46; Mark 14:34.
[29] Ps. 22:1.
[30] Ps. 22:22–28.

How does he do this? He does it in the exposition of Scripture, in the preaching of the Word of God. He fulfills his promise: "[My sheep] listen to my voice."[31] Of course, that refers in the first instance to his contemporaries. But Jesus meant much more than that. He had other "sheep" who had never literally heard his voice.[32] But they too would hear it—and recognize it.

Remember when your parents used to waken you in the morning? "It's time to get up," they said, calling you by name.

They were calling you *before* you were aware of it. At first it was simply the sound that roused you. But then you recognized you were being called by name, and then you recognized the voice, and—at least most of the time!—you got up.

Something similar happens when God's Word is expounded in the power of the Spirit. Jesus calls us. His voice awakens us spiritually. Slowly we begin to realize that he has been at work in our lives, and that he is calling us to come to him. We are disturbed out of our spiritual sleep; we are being "called" by name, and we recognize Christ's voice.

> I heard the voice of Jesus say,
> "Come unto me and rest;
> Lay down, thou weary one, lay down
> Thy head upon my breast."
> I came to Jesus as I was,
> Weary and worn and sad;
> I found in him a resting place,
> And he has made me glad.[33]

This is what happens when the Word is preached in the power of Christ. Christ himself addresses our minds, speaks to our hearts, draws out our affections, and brings us to faith and repentance.

---

[31] John 10:16.
[32] John 10:16.
[33] Horatius Bonar, "I Heard the Voice of Jesus Say," 1846.

Paul seems to be thinking about this when he writes to the Ephesians: "[Christ] came and preached peace to you who were far off and to those who were near."[34] This preaching is explicitly said to have taken place *after* Jesus had finished his work of atonement. How was it that Jesus "came and preached peace" in Ephesus? Did he ever visit Ephesus? In one sense, yes. He came and preached through the preaching of Paul and his companions!

The same point is made in Romans 10: "How can we believe in him whom we have never heard?"[35] That is the simple truth. We need to hear Christ if we are to recognize his voice and come to trust in him.

Hearing Christ

William Wilberforce, the great English Christian politician and social reformer, became a Christian at the age of twenty-five. One of his closest friends, William Pitt the Younger, became prime minister of Great Britain at the age of twenty-four.[36]

Pitt had the deepest affection for his friend but could never quite grasp what had happened to him. On one occasion Wilberforce invited him to church to hear a favorite preacher. At the close of the service Wilberforce was thrilled by the preaching. But his friend Pitt—a man of considerable intellect—turned to him and said, "Wilberforce—what was he going on about there?" They sat in the same pew; they listened to the same preacher; they heard the same sermon. But William Pitt did not hear the voice of Jesus calling him.

A man once told us that his son had been far from the Lord,

---

[34] Eph. 2:17.

[35] Verse 14. With the New American Standard Version, the ESV footnote, and a number of commentators, we take this to be the right translation—*not*, "How can we believe in him *of whom* we have never heard?" While that is a biblical truth, it is an obvious one, and probably not the specific truth Paul has in mind here. The verb he uses, "hear" (*akouo*), takes the genitive case of the person heard, not—as in English—the accusative case. So we translate "hear him," not "hear of him."

[36] Hence the ditty: "A sight to make all nations stand and stare: / A kingdom trusted to a schoolboy's care."

but one night as he came home, he "happened" to pick up a recording of a sermon we had preached. The young man listened to the sermon every day for a month. On the last day of the month, he came to a living faith in Christ. What happened? He presumably did not realize what was happening to him; Christ was calling him; only slowly did that dawn on him. He heard the same human voice again and again, but then at last he heard the voice of Christ and responded.

This is not confined to the beginnings of our Christian life. It is an ongoing reality in worship. Indeed if it were not an ongoing reality we ourselves would be inclined to abandon preaching. For without this dimension we would look out on our congregations each week, full of so many and varied needs, and simply despair. Our sermons cannot address all of these needs, nor do we have the ability to address them all in a single sermon. But when Christ comes to church and preaches his own Word, when the one who speaks to us "is able to save to the uttermost those who come to God through him"—then all needs can be met by him!

You don't come to believe in Jesus Christ until you have heard him. Until then he is simply a character in a book. But then you become conscious that there is a totally different accent speaking to you. This is why preachers find people saying to them at the church door, "Has somebody been talking to you about me?" The answer is always, "No, but perhaps *Someone* else has been talking to you about you!"

When Christ opens, or speaks through, his Word, he begins a dialogue with the soul. He engages us at the deepest level, and we bow before him to say, "Lord, Jesus, you have ministered your Word to us."

In some churches the service is divided between "worship" and "preaching" or "teaching." But there is no such division. When Christ preaches his Word to us, we know that we have been brought into communion with him, and the immediate fruit of that is the worship we bring to him during the preaching as well as before and after it.

Praise Leader

As worship leader, Jesus also leads us in our singing. Notice the words that Hebrews cites, again from Psalm 22:22: "In the midst of the congregation I will sing your praise."[37]

In one of our churches there is a lunch on Wednesdays followed by an exposition of Scripture. We look forward to it immensely because it gives us a privileged opportunity for teaching that both helps Christians and points outsiders to Christ.

One Christmas, in one of our churches, the pastors decided (by a majority!) that as part of our "Christmas present" to those who came during Christmas week we would sing a carol together. There were mixed feelings among the pastors! As the date approached, the feelings became more mixed. But just before the day itself, we arranged for our music director to rehearse us. The most reluctant pastor smiled in relief and said, "Do you mean *he is going to sing with us*?" That changed everything! No fear now of being caught singing off-key or out of tune! Now we could appear with a measure of confidence and joy to sing. His voice would cover all our faults.[38]

In true worship, Jesus is present, and he is leading the singing! We sing with him who says, "In the midst of the congregation I will sing your praise." We worship in union with Christ—and we sing in union with him too!

That puts a new light on worship. Who would not want to sing with Jesus? He makes our singing give pleasure to his Father. His singing of praise covers all the inadequacies of ours.

We need to recover an awareness of this ministry of the Lord. This is what encourages us to sing with all our heart. Jesus is stand-

---

[37] Heb. 2:12.

[38] If we mention that this particular music director had, among other roles, sung "The Voice of God" in Benjamin Britten's *Noah's Flyde*, and Dominick Argento's *Jonah and the Whale*, as well as helped to back the singer Sting, the reason for the relief will be clear!

ing among his people saying: "Father, I'm in the congregation. I'm leading the praises of your people. Listen to them singing with me. Don't you love to hear them?"

Think of this every time the service of worship begins in your church.

A graduation memory comes to mind.

One of our children studied at a collegiate university that still used only Latin throughout the graduation ceremony. One by one the various heads of the colleges led forward its graduands (wearing their undergraduate gowns) to be presented to the presiding officer. As this was done the president of the college would representatively take one of the students by the hand and introduce all his students for graduation: "Here I am and the children of my college whom I present to you in confidence for graduation." The students were then led out, still wearing their undergraduate gowns, only later to reappear wearing their graduate gowns.

Isn't that a picture of the ongoing ministry of the Lord Jesus? As we assemble together for worship, he comes by his Spirit to be the worship leader, the liturgist. He takes us by the hand and leads us into his Father's presence. We are only undergraduates in his school, but he presents us, saying, "Father, here I am, and the children you have given me! I present them to you in the confidence that you will accept their worship and bless them!"

One day we will be led into the Father's presence by Jesus. On that day we will wear graduate gowns of glory! But each Sunday, and on every other occasion we worship, we already enjoy a foretaste of it.

This is why, later in Hebrews, the author makes a staggering comparison between Old Testament worship, the prototype of which was the assembly at Sinai, and New Testament worship:

> For you have not come to what may be touched, a blazing fire and darkness and gloom and a tempest and the sound of a

trumpet and a voice whose words made the hearers beg that no further messages be spoken to them. For they could not endure the order that was given, "If even a beast touches the mountain, it shall be stoned." Indeed, so terrifying was the sight that Moses said, "I tremble with fear." But you have come to Mount Zion and to the city of the living God, the heavenly Jerusalem, and to innumerable angels in festal gathering, and to the assembly of the firstborn who are enrolled in heaven, and to God, the judge of all, and to the spirits of the righteous made perfect, and to Jesus, the mediator of a new covenant, and to the sprinkled blood that speaks a better word than the blood of Abel.[39]

This is what happens when we go to church! The risen Jesus describes this exquisitely when he says to the church in Laodicea:

Behold, I stand at the door and knock. If anyone hears my voice and opens the door, I will come in to him and eat with him, and he with me.[40]

Although these words have often been read as an evangelistic text, Jesus is actually addressing a church gathered for worship. He is talking about coming to their church, perhaps even about his presence at their Communion service.

When the Lord comes to us in this way, we are caught up into his presence and we praise him. We become conscious of his glory as his Word is ministered to us, and we begin to understand that he is not only the preacher of the Word and the leader of our praises; he is also, and supremely, the shepherd of our souls. Because he has suffered in our flesh and blood and been tempted and overcome, we know he is a priest who understands our weakness. Because he is with us, we can go to him. We know he is able to save to the uttermost everyone—anyone—who comes to God through him. And

---

[39] Heb. 12:18–24.
[40] Rev. 3:20.

we know he wants to, because he calls us his children: "Here am I and the children you have given me."[41]

What are you suffering? How are you being tested? Perhaps you feel nobody knows what you are going through, nobody could possibly understand, nobody has been where you are. You might be a young person who feels your parents and brothers and sisters don't understand you, and so you say, "Jesus would never understand me. My parents, my brothers and sisters—they don't understand me. Nobody does! And nobody cares!"

But Jesus' parents didn't understand him. His brothers and sisters and friends—none of them understood him. "People are against me," you say. People were against him. "Nobody understands me." Nobody understood him.

Someone reading these pages may agree with all this—but still say, "Yes, but my pain is different." Perhaps it is the unspeakable pain of having been abused, molested, and possibly even raped. But think about Jesus' priestly ministry. As he became the sacrifice for our sins, he also tasted (yes—he could taste it) the spittle, the blood, and the sweat, and could feel (yes—feel) the lacerations on his back, the physical abuse. He knows what it is like to be molested, stripped, beaten, and then exposed and humiliated in public. He became "a man of sorrows and acquainted with grief."[42]

"Ah, but he was sinless!" you may say. "*That* made it different for him."

Yes, that made it different. That made the shame, the humiliation, all the more intense and distasteful for him. That's the reason he is able to help you and pastor you. He has felt your weakness and shame in every atom of his being. But he remained absolutely faithful to God. And so he is able to take you by the hand and introduce you—in all your sense of shame—to the heavenly Father.

There is even more to our Lord's ongoing ministry than this.

---

[41] Heb. 2:13.
[42] Isa. 53:3.

He has been made like us in every respect.[43] He can sympathize with us in our weakness because he has been tempted in every way like us.[44] Even more, "he always lives to make intercession for them," and so "he is able to save to the uttermost."[45] That means he is also able to save you *from* "the uttermost"—whatever that might be in your life. He holds his children with one hand, and he holds on to his Father with the other hand, and as he draws near to him, he says, "Father here am I and the children you have given to me."

Many contemporary Christians have come to appreciate the hymn "Before the Throne of God Above":

Before the throne of God above
I have a strong and perfect plea.
A great high Priest whose Name is Love
Who ever lives and pleads for me.
My name is graven on His hands,
My name is written on His heart.
I know that while in Heaven He stands
No tongue can bid me thence depart.[46]

But the reality of gospel worship is that this same Jesus, by the power of the Spirit, is also present with us.

Have you ever come to Jesus, trusted him, and said, "My sins, Lord Jesus! You are the only one who can set my guilty conscience free, break the bondage of my soul, bring me into your presence, and help me to praise, glorify, and enjoy God forever"?

Jesus will do all this simultaneously. What a Savior!

---

[43] Heb. 2:17–18.
[44] Heb. 4:15.
[45] Heb. 7:25.
[46] Paradoxically, the hymn has been so widely sung to the contemporary setting by Vicki Cook that it is not always appreciated that the hymn itself is "traditional," having been written in the mid-nineteenth century by Charitie Lee Bancroft.

4

Jesus Christ,
the Conquering King

"Now after John was arrested, Jesus came into Galilee, proclaiming the gospel of God, and saying, 'The time is fulfilled, and the kingdom of God is at hand; repent and believe in the gospel'" (Mark 1:14–15). The ministry of Jesus began with this announcement.

Jesus often spoke about the kingdom of God—it is a central theme in his message. He both preached and demonstrated that the kingdom of God had broken into the world in his coming. In his preaching he taught his disciples how to enter the kingdom and the kind of lifestyle to which this would lead. Through his miracles he gave visual, physical demonstration of the restoring and transforming power of the kingdom.

A week or so prior to his crucifixion he did something that made it clear that he himself was the king in the kingdom of God. Here is John's description of the event:

> The next day the large crowd that had come to the feast heard that Jesus was coming to Jerusalem. So they took branches of palm trees and went out to meet him, crying out, "Hosanna! Blessed is he who comes in the name of the Lord, even the King of Israel!" And Jesus found a young donkey and sat on it, just as it is written,

> "Fear not, daughter of Zion;
> behold, your king is coming,
>   sitting on a donkey's colt!"

> His disciples did not understand these things at first, but when Jesus was glorified, then they remembered that these things had been written about him and had been done to him. The crowd that had been with him when he called Lazarus out of the tomb and raised him from the dead continued to bear witness. The reason why the crowd went to meet him was that they heard he had done this sign. So the Pharisees said to one another, "You see that you are gaining nothing. Look, the world has gone after him."[1]

These melodic lines in the Bible's portrayal of Jesus—the seed of the woman, the prophet, and the priest—not only run all the way from Genesis through Revelation, but they also, in a sense, intersect with one another.

You might think of these various themes in terms of a Venn diagram, those interlocking circles we learned about in math in high school. The point at which they all meet with one another centers on the person of the Lord Jesus Christ and on his work of salvation and restoration.

As boys in Sunday school, our teachers constantly reminded us that the Bible is a book all about Jesus:

- In the Old Testament Jesus is *predicted.*
- In the Gospels Jesus is *revealed.*
- In the Acts of the Apostles Jesus is *preached.*
- In the Letters Jesus is *explained.*
- In the book of Revelation Jesus is *expected.*

Actually that's quite a useful little summary for grown-ups as well as youngsters! It may not be exhaustive or sophisticated, but it cer-

---

[1] John 12:12–19.

tainly helps us as we move around the Bible. For the truth is that the Bible will be an impenetrable mystery at every point where we take our eyes away from Christ. We will lose our way around the Bible when we fail to look to Jesus.

The story of Jesus' entry into Jerusalem on the first Palm Sunday is a case in point. What is happening in this familiar passage?

Sometimes the most familiar verses can be the occasion for our most superficial reading. This particular passage is routinely read on Palm Sunday. But despite our familiarity with the Triumphal Entry scene, we may not have grasped its significance.

So—what is the message? What does it mean? Why does it matter?

Slow Learners

If we are honest about our uncertainty, we should not be unduly disheartened. We are in good company—with Jesus' own disciples. John says: "His disciples did not understand these things at first."[2] Hardly complimentary to them, is it?

Incidentally, one of the marks of the authenticity of the Gospels is, surely, the number of times the authors tell us what the disciples didn't know! They were not written to commend to the church the natural gifts of the apostles!

It is helpful—and can be wonderfully encouraging—to notice these little details. They remind us that we are on a pilgrimage, and we have not yet arrived at our destination. Jesus is transforming us, but our lives are still under construction. We too have much to learn. That simply underscores what a privilege it is to be able to possess Scripture and to live under its tutelage.

The disciples just weren't getting it, were they? Nor was this the only time John recorded their lack of spiritual intelligence.

Later, in the upper room, Jesus told them, "I am going to pre-

---

[2] John 12:16.

pare a place for you, I will come back and I will take you to be where I am," and he added: "and you know the way to where I am going." Then Thomas said, "But we don't! We don't understand you, Jesus. We don't know where you're going, so how can we know the way?" Jesus replies, "Well, you know, I am the way, and if you really knew me you'd know the Father." And then dear Philip says, "Well, Jesus, why don't you just show us the Father, and that will be enough for us." He still did not understand that the Father was revealing himself in Jesus! "Have I been with you so long," replied the Lord, "and you still do not know me, Philip? Whoever has seen me has seen the Father."[3]

Jesus tells them that they should be encouraged by the fact that when the Spirit of truth comes, he will guide them into all truth. He will not speak on his own; he will speak only what he hears, and he will tell you what is yet to come. In "a little while . . . you will see me no longer; and again a little while, and you will see me."[4] That's not particularly difficult, is it? "I'm going to be going away, and you won't see me. And then I'll be coming back, and you will see me." But some of his disciples said to one another, "What is this that he says to us, 'A little while, and you will not see me, and again a little while, and you will see me?'"[5]

Of course it seems perfectly plain to us, because we have been able to read the end of the story. We have the New Testament Letters to explain it all to us. But as you listen to the disciples, it isn't a surprise to discover that later Jesus is calling out, in prayer, "Father! Father!"—as if he is saying: "Look at these characters you have given me. I've had them in Sunday school for three years, and they're still absolutely hopeless! One after another they keep asking me these simple and basic questions. O, Father, I have kept them. Will you please keep them?"[6]

---

[3] See John 14:1–11.
[4] John 16:16.
[5] John 16:17.
[6] See John 17:11–15.

All of this underlines for us that when we read the Scriptures we need to guard ourselves from thinking, "Oh, I know a lot about this; I know all about the meaning of this passage. It's the Palm Sunday passage. I know that one. Yes, we've done that one already. I've been at any number of Palm Sunday services. There can't be anything for me to learn now. Now, Jesus, he's a king, isn't he?"

No! Our starting place should be, "Lord, you know, I really don't know much about this." Then we're more likely to think: "I wonder, what is exciting and dramatic and interesting here, and what I can discover that's fresh this morning out of this passage?"

Use Your Imagination

If it were possible for us to go back in time and observe a family preparing for the Passover, we might overhear a conversation between a boy and his father:

> "Dad, I can't wait for tomorrow. I've already got my palm branches, Dad. I'm all ready. I don't know if I'm going to be able to sleep tonight, Dad. Because tomorrow . . . it's that wonderful time, isn't it?"
>
> "Oh, yes, son. It is," the father replies.
>
> "Father, sing me a song before I go to sleep. Can we sing together that one I like?"
>
> "Which one do you mean?"
>
> "Well, isn't it one of those Psalms of Ascent?[7] The one that begins, 'I rejoiced with those who said to me . . . ' That one about how our feet are standing inside Jerusalem! Can we sing that one?"

You may know this psalm in Isaac Watts's version:

> How pleased and blest was I
> To hear the people cry,

---

[7] Psalms 120–134 seem to belong together as a kind of songbook for pilgrims at the Jerusalem festivals.

"Come, let us seek our God today!"
Yes, with a cheerful zeal
We haste to Zion's hill,
And there our vows and honors pay.[8]

It is important for us to keep in mind that the material in the
Gospels is set within the warp and woof of ordinary life. Granted,
we see this little boy only in our imaginations; but many excited little
boys just like him were there with their families on Palm Sunday—
like children lining the streets for a presidential inauguration or a
British coronation. The Jerusalem crowds, however, gathered to celebrate God's saving interventions in their nation's past. They had also
learned from the Old Testament of a new age, a new day that would
dawn, when all that had been lost and forfeited would be restored and
when all that they longed to see would be revealed. In the crowd of
bystanders and palm branch wavers, there would be multiple layers
of anticipation built into the expectation and enjoyment of that day.

Behind the Scenes

In John's record of the Triumphal Entry, however, the immediate context for what happens on Palm Sunday is the raising of Lazarus from
the dead. Jesus had come to the village of Bethany a few days after
Lazarus had died. He had gone to his tomb—probably a cave—and
had told some men to roll the stone away, and had called, "Lazarus,
come forth!" His dead friend had come walking out of the grave.
More likely he "tottered out"—he was still bound in his grave clothes.

When Lazarus came out of the tomb, Jesus gave a command
that his grave clothes should be removed. Then we are told that
many of the Jews who were there to visit Mary, and had seen what
Jesus did, put their faith in him. That is followed by the frustration
of the religious leaders, which leads to the hatching of a plot to kill
Jesus.[9] Can you imagine the "buzz" there was in this community?

---

[8] Isaac Watts's "How Pleased and Blest Was I" is a paraphrase of Psalm 122.
[9] See John 11:44–45, 48, 53.

They kept looking for Jesus, and as they stood in the temple area they asked one another,

> What do you think? That he will not come to the feast at all?[10]

But a few verses later on, when Jesus had returned to Bethany, we are told that by the time the large crowd of Jews found out that he was there,

> they came, not only on account of him but also to see Lazarus, whom he had raised from the dead.[11]

But this was not all that was happening. Because of this

> the chief priests made plans to put Lazarus to death as well, because on account of him many of the Jews were going away and believing in Jesus.[12]

What a remarkable statement! Small wonder that Jesus had looked over Jerusalem and said:

> Would that you, even you, had known on this day the things that make for peace! But now they are hidden from your eyes.[13]

Think of it. All of these people, with their deeply religious background, with their amazing heritage, with their knowledge of the Scriptures—but as they tried to weave together the strands of their messianic expectation, they got it all dreadfully wrong. Here, in the most unexpected way, is the answer to all their expectations; but they could not recognize him. Truly "he came to his own, and his own people did not receive him."[14]

It would take us on too long a journey to show how they mis-

---

[10] John 11:56.
[11] John 12:9.
[12] John 12:10–11.
[13] Luke 19:42.
[14] John 1:11.

read hint after hint, prophecy after prophecy, as the Old Testament pointed to Jesus. But it is worth pausing to set out some pointers.

The Big Picture

One of the *disadvantages* about digital—in distinction from Polaroid—cameras is that we do not get any pictures *in our hands*. Not actual pictures. But one of the *advantages* is in being able to immediately create a collage and to see how the individual moments are all part of an extended narrative leading up to the final frame. We can look back on a complete vacation or the growth of a child from kindergarten to high school. The same is true of video. We can zip through all kinds of scenes that help to explain how we reached the final scene.

In the same way, as we scroll through the Scriptures we discover the layers that precede the moment in time when Jesus arrives in Jerusalem as king.

For example, we could scroll back to Luke 1:26–38 and the appearance of the angel Gabriel to Mary. Remember how she was troubled at the greeting, and the angel said, "You shouldn't really be troubled":

> You have found favor with God. And behold, you will conceive in your womb and bear a son, and you shall call his name Jesus. He will be great and will be called the Son of the Most High. And the Lord God [notice that!] will give to him the throne of his father David, and he will reign over the house of Jacob forever, and of his kingdom there will be no end."[15]

This is one of those little snapshots. Here we have the announcement of a future birth. But there is so much more—including the nature and identity of the child who is going to be born. He will be given the throne of his father David. He is a king, and he will have a kingdom!

---

[15] Luke 1:30–33.

Mary was an ordinary young woman, probably a teenager. Small wonder that she pondered these things![16] She must have mulled them over many a day. Think of Mary watching her Jesus grow, seeing him coming back into the house after being outside, and asking him, "What have you been up to today, Jesus?" Think of her watching him in his little triumphs when he had copied the work of Joseph and so on. And always at the back of her mind the echo of the angelic announcement, "And he will reign on the throne of his father David."

Phillips Brooks captures something of that in his Christmas carol:

> O little town of Bethlehem,
> How still we see thee lie,
> Above thy deep and dreamless sleep
> The silent stars go by.
> Yet in thy dark streets shineth
> The everlasting Light;
> The hopes and fears of all the years
> Are met in thee tonight.[17]

Here it is! All the hopes and fears, all the anticipations, all the dreams, all the Old Testament promises of the one who would come and embody the great prophetic announcements about the Messiah—they are now all somehow coming to fulfillment there in Bethlehem.

And then—fast-forward thirty years—to find the same thing in this triumphant scene on the road up to Jerusalem. The King is coming!

Here is the fulfillment of the prophecy of Zechariah: "Rejoice greatly, O daughter of Zion! . . . Your king is coming to you."[18] And

---

[16] Luke 2:19.
[17] The opening verse of Phillips Brooks's hymn "O Little Town of Bethlehem," 1867.
[18] Zech. 9:9.

of Isaiah 32: "Behold, a king will reign in righteousness."[19] And of 2 Samuel 7 and the promise that God gave to David that an eternal and universal king would come from his line.[20]

All of these we discover by scrolling through the biblical record. Further back to Genesis 49 we read the prophetic words of Jacob as he blesses his sons:

> The scepter shall not depart from Judah, nor the ruler's staff from between his feet, until tribute comes to him; and to him shall be the obedience of the peoples.[21]

Now, imagine an Old Testament believer reading these—and many more—passages. They would naturally ask, "How will this be? Who can this be?"[22] As we move forward through the Bible, we find the people longing for a king, hoping that this will be the answer to all their dilemmas. But none of the kings fulfills their expectations; none of them is able to bring real salvation. And so the Old Testament people were left at the end of it all looking for the "Someone" who would be the great king. The prophetic ministry of the entire Old Testament ends with silence—several hundred years of silence—waiting for this unknown Someone who would come to be the embodiment of the prophetic word.

All this and more is on the hard drive of God's unfolding revelation, and then we come to the picture to which all the others have been pointing.

What Kind of King?

Jesus mounts a donkey and rides into Jerusalem surrounded by this huge, noisy crowd. We do not have any other record of Jesus riding anywhere, do we? This is the only place it happens.

---

[19] Isa. 32:1.
[20] 2 Sam. 7:12–16; cf. Ps. 72:1–19.
[21] Gen. 49:10.
[22] See 1 Pet. 1:10–12.

It isn't because Jesus is tired that he is riding on the donkey. He had deliberately sent his disciples into the city to get it on this particular day.[23] He wanted to make a point.

But what point?

Jesus is here confronting the community by his actions. He is deliberately entering the jurisdictions of Annas and Caiphas the Jewish high priests, and of the Jewish ruling council (the Sanhedrin), and of Pontius Pilate the governor who represented all the might of the Roman Empire. Later, Pilate will ask him, "Who in the world are you?" At one point he will ask directly, "Are you then the King of the Jews? Let's just get this sorted out, Jesus. Are you the King of the Jews?" And Jesus replies, "You have said so."[24]

But what kind of king is he? What kind of king rides on a donkey? What kind of king wears a crown that is woven with thorns? What kind of king is dressed up in someone else's robe and made to look foolish and a figure of fun and is cruelly mocked by his ill-disciplined military custodians?[25] Here we see the great paradox that confronts any intelligent reader of the Bible.

It is also the paradox that threw off many of the people who were looking for the coming one. They cried, "Save us, we pray, O LORD! O LORD, we pray, give us success!"[26] But then they witnessed a whole series of scenes in which Jesus was "despised and rejected . . . a man of sorrows . . . acquainted with grief."[27] What possibility was there that he could bring salvation, safety, and success when he could not apparently secure his own safety? His ministry had led him to such an ignominious end.

How Does Jesus Reign?

The Shorter Catechism is famous because of its opening question: "What is the chief end of man?" (Answer: "Man's chief end is to

---

[23] Matt. 21:1–11.
[24] Matt. 27:11.
[25] John 19:1–3.
[26] Ps. 118:25.
[27] Isa. 53:3.

glorify God and to enjoy him forever.")[28] But later in its exposition of the gospel it asks another important question, this time about Jesus:

> How doth Christ execute the office [ministry] of a king?

That is precisely the question these scenes force us to ask. Here is the Catechism's answer:

> In subduing us to himself, in ruling and defending us, and in restraining and conquering all his and our enemies.[29]

We have considered how Christ came as a prophet to oust our ignorance and as a priest to deal with our alienation and to lead us into God's presence. Now we see him as a king who subdues all the tyrannical forces that are arraigned against us, and, yes, those that fight within us too.

But how does King Jesus do this? Here we must limit our discussion to three dimensions and consider each of them in summary form. First, how he is king in relation to our salvation, then in relation to the cosmos, and finally in relation to the future.

Salvation

How does Jesus exercise his reign for our salvation? We will need to consider this further when we think about him as the Son of Man. But for the moment we need to understand that the cross is the crisis point of his reign. There he accomplished everything necessary to deal with our sin:

> And you, who were dead in your trespasses and the uncircumcision of your flesh, God made alive together with him, having

---

[28] Published in 1648 by the Westminster Assembly and used thereafter in many churches, especially, but not exclusively, in the Presbyterian tradition.
[29] *The Shorter Catechism*, Question 24.

forgiven us all our trespasses, by canceling the record of debt that stood against us with its legal demands. This he set aside, nailing it to the cross. He disarmed the rulers and authorities and put them to open shame, by triumphing over them in him.[30]

Earlier in his ministry the apostle Paul explained to the Galatians that this—death on a cross—meant that Jesus had borne the curse that we deserve for our sin.[31]

More than this, Jesus has done everything necessary to deliver us from the power of death.

The tyranny of sin and guilt is made visible in our death. God had said to Adam and Eve, "In the day that you eat of it [the tree of the knowledge of good and evil] you shall surely die."[32] That is now our inherited condition. Our death is the corrosive, degenerative impact of sin and judgment. The weakness, frailty, disintegration, and loss involved in death are the final evidences in this world that we have sinned and fallen short of the glory of God.

But, in addition, listen to what the author of Hebrews has to say:

> Since therefore the children share in flesh and blood, he himself likewise partook of the same things, that through death he might destroy the one who has the power of death, that is, the devil, and deliver all those who through fear of death were subject to lifelong slavery.[33]

So Jesus has done everything that we needed to be saved *from sin*. He has done everything we needed in order for us to be saved *from the judgment of death*. And he has done everything necessary to set us free *from the bondage of the Devil*. In a word, he has done everything we need done for us but could never do for ourselves.

---

[30] Col. 2:13–15.
[31] Gal. 3:13.
[32] Gen. 2:17.
[33] Heb. 2:14–15.

The evidence for his victory is, of course, the resurrection. It is like a loud "amen" being pronounced on his work by his Father.

Jesus was raised physically from the dead as a sign that his sacrifice for sin had been accepted. It was as if the Judge were saying, "You have paid the penalty the law demanded; you are now free to go!" Clearly it was also the sign that he had broken the power of death, because it was not possible for him to be held in its grip.[34]

Having crushed the power of Satan, Jesus then spent a period of forty days meeting with his disciples. What a seminar on biblical teaching and resurrection life that must have been! Imagine being taught about new life, resurrection life, by the one who had said, "I am the resurrection and the life. Whoever believes in me, though he die, yet shall he live. Whoever, and everyone who lives and believes in me shall never die."[35]

But how is it that Jesus' resurrection leads to the resurrection of those who believe in him? How can it be—as Scripture makes clear—that because Jesus rose from the grave, it is an ontological impossibility for believers not to be raised?

Here is the biblical logic:

- We are "in Christ."
- We are therefore united to him.
- We can never be separated from Christ.
- Christ has been raised from the dead.
- Therefore, because we are in him we have been raised and we will be raised![36]

This is why his resurrection is described as the "firstfruits"—it is the pledge and assurance of a final harvest.[37]

So, Jesus reigns as king in our salvation.

---

[34] Acts 2:24.
[35] John 11:25.
[36] Rom. 6:5.
[37] 1 Cor. 15:20.

The Cosmos

Scripture teaches us to think of the kingly reign of Christ in cosmic terms. Here a key text is Colossians 1:15–17: "He is the image of the invisible God, the firstborn of all creation. For by him all things were created, in heaven and on earth."

Just think about this in relation to the average class in anthropology at almost any secular university. Or think about our young students who are reading history, or those who are studying medicine and will become physicians. Does it make any difference *there* to be a Christian? Does it affect their view of things?

Does it? If Paul's words mean anything, it certainly does:

> For by him all things were created, in heaven and on earth, visible and invisible, whether thrones or dominions or rulers or authorities—all things were created through him and for him. And he is before all things, and in him all things hold together.[38]

There is, then, this great cosmic dimension to the kingship of Jesus. He is the source, the sustainer, and the goal of all created reality. "The universe was made by Him, is providentially sustained by Him and is utterly dependent on Him."[39]

As Christians we must learn to think properly, biblically. Then we may watch CNN or BBC News, or read the *New York Times*, or make our way through the *Wall Street Journal* without joining the ranks of the gloomy or singing in the choir of the fearful. To be in Christ is mind stretching and life transforming. It is a mind-altering experience to bow before the authority of what is said concerning this cosmic Christ, who reigns over all. It changes our perspective on everything.

We were not stellar students in the physics class in high school. Our report cards at the end of the year contained such statements

---

[38] Col. 1:16–17.
[39] David Wells, *What Is the Trinity?* Basics of the Faith (Philipsburg, NJ: P&R, 2012), 8–9.

as: "He has decided that physics is not for him—and he is very firm in this decision." But although we are in dangerous territory when it comes to science, we are able to look up at the night sky, and see the stars and planets, and stare in wonder at the Milky Way.

If the Milky Way contains, as astronomers now tell us, three hundred to four hundred billion stars, and if it is only one galaxy among possibly hundreds of billions of galaxies—then we little people are in need of Colossians 1:16–17 just to be able to get to bed at night and to wake up in the morning and feel we have any security at all in the universe.

We are helped by reading the prophet Isaiah's great words:

> Lift up your eyes on high and see:
> who created these?
> He who brings out their host by number,
> calling them all by name.[40]

And by this reminder from the prologue to the Gospel of John:

> All things were made through him, and without him was not any thing made that was made.[41]

In a cosmos of otherwise impenetrable mystery, we are greatly helped by knowing that Jesus is king in the cosmos.

The Future

In addition to seeing Christ's kingship salvifically and cosmically, we also need to think of it in futuristic terms.

Go back to the earlier illustration of the Venn diagram with its circles. We now begin to see how the various biblical descriptions of the Lord Jesus intersect with each another. The same Bible themes and passages keep recurring.

---

[40] Isa. 40:26.
[41] John 1:3.

So in 1 Corinthians 15, we discover that there is an order to resurrection. First, Christ the first fruits, then, when he comes, those who belong to him.

> Then comes the end, when he delivers the kingdom to God the Father after destroying every rule and every authority and power. For he must reign until he has put all his enemies under his feet. The last enemy to be destroyed is death.[42]

See then this magnificent tapestry into which images of Christ as the ascended king are woven. Truly, "the head that once was crowned with thorns is crowned with glory now."[43]

The "spillage" from his ascension is seen in the outpouring of the Holy Spirit so that he indwells the people of God. Jesus ascended in order to ask his Father to keep his promise to send the Spirit to his people so that they might experience every spiritual blessing.[44] When he, the Holy Spirit, comes, he makes much of the Word of God in our lives and points us constantly to the Son of God.[45] All this comprises the glorious benefits of Christ's triumph and kingship.

This—with all of these elements included—ought to be central in our thinking as Christians. Indeed this future dimension should control our perspective on everything, and certainly the way in which we view the world.

But how should the Christian view the world?

Worldview

The Christian views the world in terms of "the good, the bad, *and the new, and the perfect*." Yes—the new and the perfect!

When God created the cosmos he made everything in it. And he made everything good. Then came the fall of man, and every-

---

[42] 1 Cor. 15:24–26.
[43] Thomas Kelly, "The Head That Once Was Crowned with Thorns," 1820.
[44] See John 14:16–17, a promise that lies behind Acts 2:33.
[45] See John 16:14–15.

thing went bad. But in the Lord Jesus Christ it is made new. Indeed, says Paul, "If anyone is in Christ, he is a new creation."[46] More literally what he says is, "If any in Christ—new creation." In Christ's resurrection there took place a renewal process that will eventually involve the whole cosmos. "The creation itself will be set free from its bondage to corruption."[47]

We live in anticipation of the day the new creation will be realized in all its perfection. Then those who are underneath Christ's footstool will at last fall down, along with many more, and acknowledge that he is king.[48]

So we may learn to begin the day affirming that "Christ is King. Jesus is Lord!" It is important to develop the practice of affirming central gospel truths as we waken to the new day, saying to ourselves, "The Lord God omnipotent reigns. This is the twenty-fifth of January (or whatever); today the Lord God omnipotent reigns. Yes, I saw the *New York Times* before I went to sleep last night. I have it on my iTouch. I did look at the BBC report before I went to bed last night. I saw all about Gaza. I saw all about Zimbabwe. I saw so much to disturb and distress. But Christ reigns from the beginning of the day to its end—every single day of my life."

This is why we love to sing at the end of the day:

The day Thou gavest, Lord, is ended,
The darkness falls at Thy behest;
To Thee our morning hymns ascended,
Thy praise shall sanctify our rest.

We thank Thee that Thy church, unsleeping,
While earth rolls onward into light,
Through all the world her watch is keeping,
And rests not now by day or night.

---

[46] 2 Cor. 5:17.
[47] Rom. 8:21.
[48] Phil. 2:10–11.

As o'er each continent and island
The dawn leads on another day,
The voice of prayer is never silent,
Nor dies the strain of praise away.

The sun that bids us rest is waking
Our brethren 'neath the western sky,
And hour by hour fresh lips are making
Thy wondrous doings heard on high.[49]

What an amazing picture that is! Here are God's people throughout the world. And as those in one time zone are going to sleep, those in another time zone are waking. And as they do, they are saying, "The Lord God omnipotent reigns. Here I am in North Korea. I can hardly function in many areas of my life, but Jesus Christ is King. Here I am in Kuala Lumpur. Here I am in the heartlands of India. Here I am." And so God's people rise at every hour of the day to praise him in every time zone in the world. Why? Because he reigns.

And then comes the final, triumphant stanza:

So be it, Lord; Thy throne shall never,
Like earth's proud empires, pass away:
Thy kingdom stands, and grows forever,
Till all Thy creatures own Thy sway.

That's it! Earth's proud empires will all pass away. But the kingdom of Jesus Christ will continue, grow, triumph—and last forever.

Implications

Now, as we begin to grasp all this, we see that the kingship of Jesus changes the way in which we view the world. And the kingship of Jesus will then control how we live in that world.

We must not affirm that "Jesus Christ is King" or trot out

---

[49] John Ellerton, "The Day Thou Gavest, Lord, Is Ended," 1870.

phrases like "Jesus Christ is Lord" as if these are merely expressions of personal devotion. That would show that we had failed to understand their real meaning. When Paul wrote of the day when, "at the name of Jesus every knee should bow . . . and every tongue confess that Jesus Christ is Lord,"[50] he was not describing the devotion of the worshiper but the identity of the one who is worshiped. He is proclaiming the divine identity of Jesus. Jesus is Lord. This isn't a statement about *my attitude to Jesus*; it is a statement about *who Jesus is*. He is Lord. *Kurios* is the Greek word he uses. In the Greek version of the Old Testament current in Paul's world, that was the standard way of translating the great covenant name for God, "Yahweh."

And since Jesus is Lord and God, King and Savior, this impacts all of life.

For example, I have no right to develop convictions or practice a lifestyle contrary to my King's word. That is why I cannot, for example, invent new views of marriage, or reengineer human sexuality, because I bow beneath the rule of the King.

I cannot rewrite the New Testament documents. I dare not play fast and loose with the historical narrative in Genesis 1–11. Why? Because Jesus is King, and this is the King's Word. Nor do I have the right to behave in any way I please. My behavior must be marked by obedience to my King.

The reign of Jesus will also influence my business practices. It will affect the way in which I go to work tomorrow morning. It affects my relationship as a child with my parents, or as a parent with my children, or as a husband with my wife, and so on.

In addition, I have no right to think that I can be disenfranchised or disengaged from the people of God, because my Lord and King is also the head of the body, the church. It is in company with others who have been brought under his lordship that I both benefit and make a contribution.

---

[50] Phil. 2:10–11.

Not only do we obey his commands, but we also enjoy his company. He is a King who has made himself accessible and who is wonderfully approachable.

We have no right of immediate access to the British monarch in Buckingham Palace in London. But we do have immediate access to the King of kings and Lord of lords. Moreover, he is not only our King—he is our Savior. And he is not only our Savior; he is our friend! It's true: "There's not a friend like the lowly Jesus. No, not one!"[51] So we can come to him with all our fears, with all our failures, with all our stresses, with all our disappointments, with all our losses, and with all the needs of our loved ones and say, "Jesus, you're the King over all of this. There's so much that we can't handle. There are so many aspects of this that are overwhelming us. But we come before you now." And then we can rise to our feet and go out into the day—and into all of our days—to declare these great and amazing truths.

Back again to Sunday school in Scotland! Our teachers used to teach us some of the most amazing songs. They are etched into our memories—and some of them really were marvelous. Here is one that drives home the nitty-gritty, day-to-day, practical difference it makes to know that Jesus is King. In its child-friendly, child-attractive fun way (and surely children had fun with Jesus?), it underscores the power of the gospel. It says: "Come on now, you don't have to be bedeviled and overwhelmed by all of these things that are coming at you." Here are the words:

> Come leave your house on Grumble Street
> And move to Sunshine Square.
> For that's the place where Jesus lives,
> And you'll be happy there!

Well, you say, "That isn't exactly a brilliant lyric. What were they doing teaching mischievous little boys that kind of poetry?"

---

[51] Johnson Oatman, "There's Not a Friend Like the Lowly Jesus," 1895.

Yes, but we got the message of these choruses. It wasn't necessary to master a systematic theology textbook to see the point: "Come on now; we say that Jesus Christ is King. Why then are our faces sad? Jesus Christ is King. Where then is our hope? Jesus Christ is King and Lord; where is our enthusiasm for the Lord Jesus? We do need to leave our house in Grumble Street and move to Sunshine Square. That's the place where Jesus is. We'll be happy there."

And then as we grew up we learned the great "grown-up" words of Isaac Watts, in his wonderful paraphrase of Psalm 72: "Jesus shall reign where'er the sun." It has a special association for us because of the story of Eric Liddell.

In 1925 Eric Liddell was leaving Scotland to go to China as a missionary teacher. He was both a Scottish Rugby internationalist and an Olympic gold medalist in the 1924 Olympics in Paris (memorialized in the movie *Chariots of Fire*).

When Eric Liddell boarded his train in Waverley Station, Edinburgh, on the first leg of his journey to China, a vast crowd had gathered to bid him farewell. He was the great sports superstar of his day. Family and friends intermingled with folks just off the street. Liddell lowered the window of his compartment, put his head out of the window, and shouted, "Christ for the world, for the world needs Christ!" And then he led this massive throng in singing the hymn "Jesus Shall Reign Where'er the Sun."

Here is the vision of Christ's reign that the people of God have shared since time immemorial:

> Jesus shall reign where'er the sun
> Does his successive journeys run;
> His kingdom stretch from shore to shore,
> Till moons shall wax and wane no more.
>
> To Him shall endless prayer be made,
> And praises throng to crown His head;
> His Name like sweet perfume shall rise
> With every morning sacrifice.

People and realms of every tongue
Dwell on His love with sweetest song;
And infant voices shall proclaim
Their early blessings on His Name.

Blessings abound where'er He reigns;
The prisoner leaps to lose his chains;
The weary find eternal rest,
And all the sons of want are blessed.

Where He displays His healing power,
Death and the curse are known no more:
In Him the tribes of Adam boast
More blessings than their father lost.

Let every creature rise and bring
Peculiar honors to our King;
Angels descend with songs again,
And earth repeat the loud amen!

That was the 1920s in Edinburgh.[52]
    It is now a century later.
    Jesus Christ was King then.
    Jesus Christ is still King now.
    Cheer up, you saints of God.

---

[52] Eric Liddell died in a Chinese internment camp on February 21, 1945. His last reported words were, "It's complete surrender."

5

Jesus Christ,
the Son of Man

Many Christians have been familiar with the expression "Son of Man" since they were children in Sunday school. Perhaps you were taught there that since Jesus is both God and man, the Bible calls him both "Son of God" and "Son of Man."[1]

Jesus is indeed both God and man. But the title "Son of Man" means a great deal more than that Jesus was human.

Origin

The origin of Jesus' own use of this title lies partly in Daniel 7. Daniel had extraordinary, apocalyptic visions, some of them of a nightmare character. The one recorded in Daniel 7 took place in the first year of Belshazzar, the king of Babylon. Daniel saw four beasts coming out of the sea in all their horrific power. Then he looked beyond the sea into the sky. Here is what he saw:

> As I looked,
> thrones were placed,
>   and the Ancient of Days took his seat;
> his clothing was white as snow,
>   and the hair of his head like pure wool;

---

[1] This way of thinking goes back to some of the earliest Christian writers such as Justin Martyr (AD 100–165) and Irenaeus of Lyons (AD 130–200), but it is clearly a less than adequate way of thinking about the biblical teaching.

his throne was fiery flames;
    its wheels were burning fire.
A stream of fire issued
    and came out from before him;
a thousand thousands served him,
    and ten thousand times ten thousand stood before him;
the court sat in judgment,
    and the books were opened.

I looked then because of the sound of the great words that the horn was speaking. And as I looked, the beast was killed, and its body destroyed and given over to be burned with fire. As for the rest of the beasts, their dominion was taken away, but their lives were prolonged for a season and a time.

I saw in the night visions,
and behold, with the clouds of heaven
    there came one like a son of man,
and he came to the Ancient of Days
    and was presented before him.
And to him was given dominion
    and glory and a kingdom,
that all peoples, nations, and languages
    should serve him;
his dominion is an everlasting dominion,
    which shall not pass away,
and his kingdom one
    that shall not be destroyed.[2]

Some verses later, he gives us a further detailed description of this judgment scene:

"But the court shall sit in judgment,
    and his dominion shall be taken away,
    to be consumed and destroyed to the end.

---

[2] Dan. 7:9–14.

And the kingdom and the dominion
>   and the greatness of the kingdoms under the whole heaven
>   shall be given to the people of the saints of the Most High;
> their kingdom shall be an everlasting kingdom,
>   and all dominions shall serve and obey them."

Here is the end of the matter.[3]

Since we are both Scots, we have never developed the instinct to say to almost total strangers, "Do you want to see a picture of my family?" But when we look at photographs of our children over the years we sometimes notice that they have characteristics—it could be a way of standing or looking—that have been there from "way back." We are struck by how deeply embedded some of their character traits seem to be.

In the same way, when we look at the biblical "photographs" of the Lord Jesus Christ, we see what is most deeply embedded in the biblical portrait of his person and work. The picture of him as Son of Man fits into that category.

In the Gospels Jesus calls himself "the Son of Man" on about fifty *separate* occasions (not counting parallel passages). These sayings may be so familiar to us that we rarely pause to reflect on them or notice the similarities and the differences between the contexts in which they appear.

Have you, for example, ever noticed in all fifty or so times Jesus is called "the Son of Man" in the Gospels that the speaker is always—Jesus himself? Nobody else in the Gospels ever refers to him as the Son of Man.[4] Simply on the basis of these statistics we could say that "the Son of Man" was Jesus' favorite self-designation. And when you analyze the fifty separate times Jesus uses the title, it seems fairly clear that, in his mind, this was the most comprehen-

---

[3] Dan. 7:26–28.

[4] John 12:34 is only an apparent exception since the crowds are simply quoting Jesus' own words. Outside of the Gospels the only exception to the same rule is found in Stephen's wonderful words in Acts 7:56.

sive description of his identity, his work, and the significance of his ministry.

There can be very little doubt from reading his words that he saw the background to this picture of himself as the Son of Man in Daniel's vision. There are three elements in that vision.

The Coming Reign of God

The first element is a prophecy of the coming reign of God. Daniel has a vision of demonic powers being released:

> Daniel declared, "I saw in my vision by night, and behold, the four winds of heaven were stirring up the great sea. And four great beasts came up out of the sea, different from one another. The first was like a lion and had eagles' wings. Then as I looked its wings were plucked off, and it was lifted up from the ground and made to stand on two feet like a man, and the mind of a man was given to it. And behold, another beast, a second one, like a bear. It was raised up on one side. It had three ribs in its mouth between its teeth; and it was told, 'Arise, devour much flesh.' After this I looked, and behold, another, like a leopard, with four wings of a bird on its back. And the beast had four heads, and dominion was given to it. After this I saw in the night visions, and behold, a fourth beast, terrifying and dreadful and exceedingly strong. It had great iron teeth; it devoured and broke in pieces and stamped what was left with its feet. It was different from all the beasts that were before it, and it had ten horns. I considered the horns, and behold, there came up among them another horn, a little one, before which three of the first horns were plucked up by the roots. And behold, in this horn were eyes like the eyes of a man, and a mouth speaking great things."[5]

Daniel is terrified and asks: "Will somebody please give me the interpretation?" He approaches one of the strange figures in whose presence he stands "and asked him the truth."[6]

---

[5] Dan. 7:2–8.
[6] Dan. 7:15.

This is a common feature of *apocalyptic* literature. We find it again in the book of Revelation.[7] Both Daniel and the apostle John were so drawn into the reality of their visions that they seem to step into the world they are observing and become participants in their own vision. They are not just, as it were, on the outside looking in. They are there; they are watching themselves becoming part of the vision! They feel their own lives are somehow caught up in the significance of what they are watching. So they ask, "Can somebody please explain this to me?"

Daniel's vision has a meaning. These beasts are powers that will arise in the earth and ravage it. The picture is horrific. War is waged against the saints. But God's throne is fixed in heaven, and the security of the kingdom of God is established by the work of the Son of Man. He is given dominion and glory and a kingdom. And in the end "the greatness of the kingdoms under the whole heaven shall be given to the people of the saints of the Most High."[8]

So here is a graphic picture of world history as the context of conflict between the kingdom of God and the powers of darkness. It is a vision version of Genesis 3:15, isn't it? Daniel foresees times in which the powers of darkness arise with such monumental authority and destructive power that it seems likely that the kingdom of God will be sunk into the sea. But then this great assurance is given to Daniel: the kingdom of God will overwhelm all other kingdoms. It is a recurring theme in the book. Kingdoms come; kingdoms go. Empires rise and fall. But the kingdom of God will be established and will endure forevermore. The entire vision is a great picture and promise of the triumph of God.

The Certain Judgment of Evil

Second, this scene contains a marvelous prophecy of the coming judgment of evil.

---

[7] Rev. 7:13–14.
[8] Dan. 7:27.

Because we can read the Old Testament Scriptures with the 20/20 vision of New Testament sight, we know that Old Testament prophecies are sometimes fulfilled in stages. The experienced mountaineer knows that the peak he sees before him is but one stage of his ascent to the summit.

Some Old Testament visions have this characteristic. They give us a picture of God's mighty victory. But then as that victory unfolds in history, it does so in stages. There are peaks and staging posts along the way before we come finally to the summit.

This is what we find here. The kingdom of God will be established. The kingdom of darkness will be overwhelmed. But as the track of redemptive history ascends, we discover a series of peaks before the kingdom of darkness is finally annihilated.

Daniel is looking forward and upward. In his vision the victory looks like one single event. But we have now learned from the New Testament that while the kingdom of God has already come in Christ, it has not yet been consummated. We are living between two mountain peaks—one called Inauguration and the other called Consummation. One peak has already been scaled in the death, resurrection, ascension, and enthronement of the Lord Jesus. The other will be scaled finally at his return in glory.

The coming judgment of evil described by Daniel was inaugurated in the ministry of our Lord Jesus. "Now is the judgment of this world," he said; "now will the ruler of this world be cast out."[9] He is cast out by Christ's death and resurrection. But he is not yet cast into the lake of fire.[10]

Now Daniel begins to understand. He sees thrones set in heaven, and the Ancient of Days appears, seated on his throne:

> As I looked,
> thrones were placed,
>   and the Ancient of Days took his seat;

---

[9] John 12:31.
[10] Rev. 20:10.

his clothing was white as snow,
    and the hair of his head like pure wool;
his throne was fiery flames;
    its wheels were burning fire.
A stream of fire issued
    and came out from before him;
a thousand thousands served him,
    and ten thousand times ten thousand stood before him;
the court sat in judgment,
    and the books were opened.[11]

Then, from the distance, riding as it were on the clouds of heaven, the Son of Man comes to the Ancient of Days:

I saw in the night visions,
and behold, with the clouds of heaven
    there came one like a son of man,
and he came to the Ancient of Days
    and was presented before him.
And to him was given dominion
    and glory and a kingdom,
that all peoples, nations, and languages
    should serve him;
his dominion is an everlasting dominion,
    which shall not pass away,
and his kingdom one
    that shall not be destroyed.[12]

The Son of Man is coming to the source of ultimate authority. That authority did not reside then in either Jerusalem or Babylon. Nor does it reside today in Washington, DC, or in London, or in Beijing. It resides exclusively in the Ancient of Days, who is seated on the throne. But the Son of Man who comes to the Ancient of Days now shares this dominion and power and will do so forever.

---

[11] Dan. 7:9–10.
[12] Dan. 7:13–14.

As Daniel looks forward to this, and longs to understand it, he is in the same position as Isaiah, or Ezekiel, or any of the prophets. Peter describes these men. They "searched and inquired carefully, inquiring what person or time the Spirit of Christ in them was indicating when he predicted the sufferings of Christ and the subsequent glories."[13]

So we can think of Daniel like this: there he is, seeing these Technicolor, HD pictures, but he is scratching his head and asking, "Who is this Son of Man figure? When will he come? What does this all mean?"

There were so many details of the prophecy still to be fulfilled. Nevertheless, in a time of enormous stress, Daniel's soul is anchored by this great vision. Like Isaiah he has caught a glimpse of the majesty of God in heaven. And also like Isaiah he has become conscious of another, as yet unidentified, figure—in Isaiah's case, "the Suffering Servant" and in Daniel's, "the Son of Man."

When this door into heaven, through which Daniel has walked, closes again, he will be able to come back down to earth and live here and now in the light of the triumph of God. But he knows now that the Son of Man must first appear. Only after that will he go to the throne of the Most High to receive his kingdom. But for now, living as he is in Babylon in changing and troublesome times, he will be able to remember that God is on the throne and that the kingdom will be given to the Son of Man some day in the future. He has seen the books being opened, and the Ancient of Days exercising judgment, and the dominion of the beasts being destroyed. He has seen that the verdict will be given to the saints of the Most High and that they will share in the bounty of the kingdom.

The remarkable thing about this picture of Jesus is that he is never isolated from his people. That is true of each aspect of his ministry—as prophet, priest, and king—since his work is always

---

[13] 1 Pet. 1:10–11.

related to our blessing. As we shall see, his ministry as the Suffering Servant is similarly exercised on behalf of his people. And the triumph of the Son of Man described here is for the saints of the Most High. So the entire passage ends with this amazing picture:

> And the kingdom and the dominion
>> and the greatness of the kingdoms under the whole heaven
>> shall be given to the people of the saints of the Most High;
> their kingdom shall be an everlasting kingdom,
>> and all dominions shall serve and obey them.[14]

This was actually one of the very first things Jesus taught his disciples. Having proclaimed the gospel of the kingdom and shown its transforming power through his mighty works, he went on to teach his disciples about life in the kingdom. Among the first words of his Sermon on the Mount was an echo of this very vision: "Blessed are the meek, *for they shall inherit the earth.*"[15] So there are lines that run from Daniel 7 into the New Testament Scriptures as they are fulfilled in the Lord Jesus Christ.

There is a promise here of the coming reign of God. There is a promise of the coming judgment of evil.

But the third element to notice here is the key promise in this passage.

The Promise of "The Son of Man": The Significance of the Title

Given this background in Daniel 7, there is more to Jesus' use of the title "Son of Man" than a simple stress on his humanity in distinction from his deity. The picture of the vision is one of unparalleled triumph, magnificence, and, indeed, glory. The Son of Man is seen coming to the throne of the Majesty on High, the Ancient of Days, and receiving authority over the whole cosmos. The rationale for

---

[14] Dan. 7:27.
[15] Matt. 5:5.

this title cannot be that it stresses humility rather than great dignity! Somehow both are involved.

What, then, does the vision mean?

Ezekiel

In the Old Testament the expression "son of man" appears most frequently in the book of Ezekiel in the context of God personally addressing the prophet.[16] God is God, and Ezekiel is "only" a man. He must therefore entrust himself wholly to God for his mission.

But "son of man" also seems to mark out Ezekiel from others—he is a faithful man, a real man. "Son of" is a Hebrew way of saying "possessing the properties of, being characterized by, exhibiting the marks of." The expression "son of destruction" means a person for whom destruction is in character.[17]

Think of the nickname Jesus gave to James and John (perhaps he gave all the disciples such names): they were known as *Boanerges*, "Sons of Thunder." Jesus meant that these two disciples had thunder-like personalities. After all, they wanted to call down fire from heaven on the Samaritans.[18] (Simon Peter was not the only disciple with aspirations beyond his abilities!) So, when the Scriptures use the expression "son of man," one latent aspect of its meaning is: "here is a true man."

In addition, when God addresses Ezekiel as "son of man," there seems to be an undertone of affection—as an English gentleman of the eighteenth century might have addressed an intimate friend, "*My dear man*, this gift is too generous by far!" It is not God's "normal" form of address. But it is also worth noting that in Ezekiel the expression is used *without the definite article*. Ezekiel is *a* son of man, not "*the* Son of Man"! The Lord Jesus alone is *the* Son of Man.[19]

---

[16] E.g., in Ezek. 2:1, 3, 6, 8. Ninety-three out of the 107 Old Testament references are found in Ezekiel.

[17] John 17:12.

[18] Luke 9:54.

[19] The presence of the definite article ("the") before "son of man" is a fixed pattern in the Gospels. Only in John 5:27 do we find an exception.

Psalm 8

The term appears again, significantly, in Psalm 8, in the question, "What is man that you are mindful of him, and the son of man that you care for him?"[20]

Psalm 8 is a meditation on creation and on the sheer condescending goodness of God in making man as his image and in his likeness. We contribute nothing to our own existence, and yet God has lavished privileges upon us—and did so first of all on Adam.[21] The son of man is God's image, privileged to be given a kind of threefold office. He is to be the prophet who brings God's word to all creation. He is to be the priest, indeed the liturgist, who gives intelligent expression to the worship that is due from all of God's creatures. He is to be the king who will exercise his reign and dominion.

The background, therefore, to Jesus' use of the expression as a self-identifier seems to lie in the creation of Adam, the ministry of Ezekiel, and the vision of Daniel.

Jesus is the real man, or, in Martin Luther's expression "The Proper Man."[22] He is "man as he was created to be" and "the man who fulfills man's destiny."

The Big Picture

In the last analysis this is actually the big picture of the Bible. The first Adam, the first son of man, sinned and fell; Jesus is the second Man and the "last Adam."[23] Adam was created to be the son of man, to exercise dominion in the name of God. As we noted in the opening chapter, his calling was to take the little garden God had given to him and then, as lord of the *microcosmos*, to reflect God's gracious character in his dominion over the *macrocosmos*.

---

[20] Ps. 8:4.
[21] Gen. 1:26–28.
[22] Martin Luther, "A Mighty Fortress Is Our God," 1529.
[23] 1 Cor. 15:45.

In this way, God intended Adam to enjoy a "shared experience" with him that would further enhance the joy of their fellowship and their pleasure in one another, as Father and son. It was as though God were saying:

> Now Adam, so that we may enjoy each other's company, I am giving you a little taste of what I know and enjoy infinitely as Creator and Provider. So here is a little garden. I'll give you a start. I want you to be lord not only of this garden; I want you to have dominion over everything on the earth. And as that happens, you will find that you will get to know and love me even more! Plus—I'll be able to love you even more as I, your Father, watch you, my son, growing in your abilities, and in your understanding of me and your love for me. We will have so much to talk about as you grow to maturity!

In simple terms, as heavenly Father, God wanted his child to have "shared experiences" that would lead to an ever-deepening sense of fellowship with him. That would go even beyond tending and expanding the garden to sharing a "secondary act of creation" in becoming a father himself.

Think of the words of Jesus (do they, perhaps, reflect his experience in the carpenter's shop of Joseph?): "The Son can do nothing of his own accord, but only what he sees the Father doing." And later on, "I have given them the words that you gave me."[24]

That is what it means to be the Son of Man. It means to be made in God's image and to fulfill the divine destiny that would lead to a world ordered and completed as God's garden, extending to the ends of the earth.[25] So creation as God's image, fellowship with him in life, experiencing his love and affection, being given a glorious destiny—all this is wrapped up in Jesus' use of the expression "Son of Man." He is the one who will accomplish all this.

---

[24] John 5:19; 17:7–8.
[25] See Revelation 21–22 where the new Jerusalem turns out to be a garden city.

Which Direction?

But there is something additional in Daniel's vision of the son of man. When the son of man first appears in the vision, *in what direction is he going?*

That's an odd question, surely.

Look again at Daniel 7 and ask yourself the questions, when the son of man is said to *come*, in what *direction* is he *coming?* And from where?

> I saw in the night visions,
> and behold, with the clouds of heaven
>   there came one like a son of man,

Now, where has he come from and where is he going to?

> And he came to the Ancient of Days.[26]

Why is this significant?

We have a tendency to assume that whenever we read about Jesus, the Son of Man, "coming," the words refer to his *second* coming.

But Daniel 7 raises an important question. When Scripture speaks about the Son of Man coming, we need to ask: *in what direction is the Son of Man coming?* Sometimes his "coming" refers not to the end when he comes from heaven but to his post-resurrection ascension and enthronement at the right hand of his Father with all the implications and consequences of that for the establishing of his kingdom.[27]

Yes, one day Jesus will come *from* the Ancient of Days to bring in the final consummation of his kingdom. But here, the reference to the coming of the Son of Man seems to refer to Jesus' *coming to* the throne of God following his incarnation, death, resurrec-

---

[26] Dan. 7:13.
[27] Luke 24:50–53; Acts 1:9–11.

tion, and ascension. This is not Jesus' coming at the end but at the midpoint of time. He comes to his Father as one who has broken the neck of the powers of darkness, has taken the sting of death, has borne the guilt of sin, has tasted the judgment curse of God, and has risen from the grave. His "coming" is actually a "going" to the Ancient of Days, clothed in our humanity, having done all that Adam and we have failed to do, and having taken the judgment Adam and we deserve. From now on the kingdom he has regained will be shared with all of his saints.

The Early Fathers of the church used to think of Psalm 24 as envisaging this climactic moment:[28]

> Lift up your heads, O gates!
>> And be lifted up, O ancient doors,
>> that the King of glory may come in.
> Who is this King of glory?
>> The LORD, strong and mighty,
>> the LORD, mighty in battle!
> Lift up your heads, O gates!
>> And lift them up, O ancient doors,
>> that the King of glory may come in.
> Who is this King of glory?
>> The LORD of hosts,
>> he is the King of glory![29]

In their imagination these writers saw the hosts of heaven looking out from the towers of the heavenly Jerusalem to see the ascending Lord Jesus accompanied by a retinue of angels chanting, "Open the city gates and let the King of glory in!"

From the city towers comes the response, "But who is this King of glory that we should fling open the gates of the heavenly Jerusalem for him?"

---

[28] "The Early Fathers" refers to Christians from the first four or five centuries of the church whose writings are still in existence.
[29] Ps. 24:7–10.

The answer? "The Lord, strong and mighty in battle. He is the King of glory. Open the doors that the King of glory may come in!"

And so the Son of Man comes to the Ancient of Days. He comes from the bloody scenes of Calvary and the victory of his resurrection to receive the kingdom and the power and the glory. Now the nations will be undeceived by the gospel, and Jesus will build his church in this enemy-occupied (but no longer owner-occupied!) world. And the day will dawn when "every knee should bow . . . and every tongue confess that Jesus Christ is Lord, to the glory of God the Father."[30]

So the immediate focus of Daniel's vision is the completion of the earthly ministry of Jesus. Yes, he will come again in majesty and glory to end all history and bring in the new heavens and the new earth. But the focus of this vision is on the fruit of his first coming.

Surely Jesus included this passage when, as yet unrecognized, he walked along with the confused disciples on the Emmaus Road and explained the Old Testament to them. Were Cleopas and his companion as confused about the second half of Daniel as we can be? Perhaps Jesus said to them:

> Friends, I know the visions of Daniel are difficult for you to understand, and I know you may have been frightened off studying them because the rabbis have treated them like puzzles. But don't you see who this person is? Don't you see why your Master was always referring to himself as "the Son of Man"? And don't you see the connection of all this to the promise of the seed of the woman, as well as to the promise to Abraham in Genesis that in his seed the nations would be blessed, and to the promise of the second psalm: "Ask of me, Son, and I will give you the nations for your inheritance"? And don't you see that "it was necessary for the Son of Man to suffer and then enter his glory" as Isaiah 52:13–15 taught you?

---

[30] Phil. 2:10–11.

> Behold, my servant shall act wisely;
>> he shall be high and lifted up,
>> and shall be exalted.
> As many were astonished at you—
>> his appearance was so marred, beyond human
>>> semblance,
>> and his form beyond that of the children of mankind—
> so shall he sprinkle many nations;
>> kings shall shut their mouths because of him;
> for that which has not been told them they see,
>> and that which they have not heard they understand.[31]

Little did they know that this veiled one would soon teach them that all dominion in heaven and earth was his. Little did they know that soon they themselves would be sent to the ends of the earth to extend the garden of grace!"

So far, then, we have looked at the way the "Son of Man" title is found in the Old Testament and how it is ultimately fulfilled in Jesus.

The fifty or so individual sayings in which Jesus refers to himself as "Son of Man" fall essentially into three categories. A little exercise can help us more fully appreciate the significance of this. If you are in the habit of marking your Bible or have an old Bible you could mark, notice every use of "Son of Man" in the Gospels, and then highlight each saying in color according to the category to which it belongs. (Apart from anything else, you will learn a tremendous amount simply by quickly reading the Gospels as a whole!)

Category 1

"Category 1" sayings describe the incarnate Son of Man *establishing* his kingdom.

Probably the easiest place to see this is in Matthew 4 through 7. Here, as we will see, Jesus is the Son of Man entering into conflict

---

[31] Isa. 52:13–15; see also Gen. 3:15; 12:1–3; Ps. 2:8; Luke 24:13–35.

with the powers of darkness. He has come to bring judgment. As Luther put it:

> For us fights the Proper Man
> Whom God himself hath bidden.[32]

Or, in a different church tradition, as John Henry Newman wrote:

> O loving wisdom of our God,
> When all was sin and shame
> A second Adam to the fight
> And to the rescue came.
>
> O wisest love, that flesh and blood
> That did in Adam fail
> Should strive afresh against the foe
> Should strive and should prevail.[33]

Matthew's Account

Matthew's Gospel is very instructive in this context. It has a distinctive shape as it proceeds from Matthew 3:13 through Matthew 7:29. It moves from (1) Jesus' baptism in the Jordan in which he enters the public phase of his ministry as God's Son, the last Adam, and the Messiah. This is followed by (2) the temptation to seize the kingdom by avoiding the cross. Emerging victorious, he now (3) begins to proclaim the coming of his kingdom, and (4) demonstrates its presence by healing the sick and pressing back the powers of darkness. This then leads to (5) his exposition of the kingdom lifestyle in the Sermon on the Mount.

1) *Baptism.* John the Baptist proclaimed that the kingdom was at hand and that people should repent. As people responded, "they were baptized by him in the river Jordan, confessing their sins."[34]

---

[32] Luther, "A Mighty Fortress Is Our God."

[33] From John Henry Newman's poem "Dream of Gerontius."

[34] Matt. 3:6.

But when Jesus came to be baptized, John argued with him. He, the Baptist, needed to be baptized by Jesus, not the other way round. John knew he was a sinner and that Jesus was the (spotless) "Lamb of God."[35] But that was exactly the point. Only if the spotless one was baptized into fellowship with sinners could sinners in turn be baptized into the fellowship of the sin bearer and experience the forgiveness of sin.

But kingdom grace brings more than forgiveness. It brings freedom from the powers of darkness and restoration to new life. Hence Jesus moves inexorably from baptism to conflict with Satan.

2) *Temptations.* In Matthew's account, the last and climactic of the three temptations is about the kingdom:

> Again, the devil took him to a very high mountain and showed him all the kingdoms of the world and their glory. And he said to him, "All these I will give you, if you will fall down and worship me." Then Jesus said to him, "Be gone, Satan! For it is written,
>
> > 'You shall worship the Lord your God
> > and him only shall you serve.'"[36]

Why would that be a temptation to Jesus? Would he not just smile and say, "That's no temptation to me"? It was a real temptation because regaining the kingdoms of this world from Satan was precisely the mission on which his Father had sent him. That is why he was incarnate as the second Man, the last Adam, and the Son of Man!

Satan was prepared to offer Jesus exactly what his Father had commanded him to recover. But the price was the same as Adam and Eve so foolishly and short-sightedly paid in the garden of Eden: disobedience. The Devil was a liar and deceiver from the beginning, and now he sought to deceive Jesus. The temptation

---

[35] John 1:29.
[36] Matt. 4:8–10.

was real because the prize was right. But our Lord saw through the deceit. Had he bowed down, the entire cosmos would be forever lost. If he had snatched at the kingdoms of this world, which he had come to regain righteously, all would be lost.

When Jesus rebukes Satan with the words, "Be gone, Satan!"[37] he speaks with all the authority of the divinely ordained prophet and the God-appointed king. He is delivering the first truly destructive blow the kingdom of darkness has ever experienced.

We need to understand this has never before been done in human history. Jesus is the second Man. There has been no one between Adam and Jesus able to do this. This is what the first man was supposed to do.

Perhaps this is why the Serpent did not go to Adam directly. If instead he could ensnare God's very best gift to Adam, namely Eve, he knew he would gain far more leverage to destroy Adam's work. The first man was supposed to crush the head of the Serpent. He failed at every point. But what Adam the first failed to do, Adam the last, Jesus Christ, came to accomplish.

This is why Mark's Gospel—which describes the temptations of Jesus only briefly—includes this significant detail: Jesus was in *the wilderness*, surrounded by *wild beasts*.[38] Unlike Adam, Jesus was not surrounded by beautiful trees and by animals he himself had named (an act that expresses authority over them). He was hungry and thirsty, and he was in a barren wilderness, surrounded by "nature red in tooth and claw."[39]

Nobody had withstood Satan thus far before. Nobody had been able to bear this level of temptation before. Yes, there was more to undergo. But for the very first time, Satan had to retreat. We could apply to Jesus' triumph here (and elsewhere) the famous words of Neil Armstrong, the first man to set foot on the moon:

---

[37] Matt. 4:10.
[38] Mark 1:12–13.
[39] The expression comes from Alfred Lord Tennyson's poem "In Memoriam."

"One small step for a man—a giant leap for mankind." In the wilderness, Christ broke a gaping hole in Satan's kingdom.

3) *Kingdom proclamation*. Notice what Jesus does next: he begins to preach, "Repent, for the kingdom of heaven is at hand."[40] And then he calls people into his kingdom. He comes to one person after another and says, "Leave your fishing boats and your nets and follow me."

4) *Kingdom demonstration*. So Jesus establishes his kingdom. He proclaims his kingdom. He brings disciples into his kingdom. Then he begins to manifest the power of his kingdom. He goes throughout Galilee. He heals the sick and delivers those whose lives have been oppressed by the powers of darkness. His fame spreads, and "they brought him all the sick, those afflicted with various diseases and pains, those oppressed by demons, epileptics, and paralytics, and he healed them."[41] What is the meaning of this? Jesus is now exercising his authority in the light of his triumph; he is setting free prisoners of war. He is beginning the divine work of restoration. He has the power to throw the effects of sin into reverse gear.

The essence of Jesus' miracles of healing and transformation is that they are signs. But signs of what? They point to the final regeneration and resurrection of the cosmos that the Lord Jesus Christ will bring in at the end, when he makes all things new.

This final kingdom, which will be on display then, has erupted in his ministry and is already visible in his victory over the powers of darkness and his reversal of the effects of sin. To the same man he says, "Your sins are forgiven," and, "Rise, pick up your bed and go home."[42] The spiritual and physical effects of the fall are reversed in one and the same miracle.

Already Jesus is giving glimpses of the future renewed creation. Perhaps you have gone into a darkened room and switched on the

---

[40] Matt. 4:17.
[41] Matt. 4:23–25.
[42] Matt. 9:1–8.

light, only for it to fuse. Yet in that moment you caught a glimpse of what was in the room. In a similar way the miracles give us momentary glimpses of the last and future world when all things will be made new.

Jesus' miracles were acts of deep compassion. But more than that, they pointed to his identity as the Son of Man who is establishing his kingdom in the world and showing its power.

5) *Kingdom lifestyle*. What immediately follows in the Gospel of Matthew is the Sermon on the Mount. "Seeing the crowds"—the words connect Matthew 4 and 5—what does Jesus do next? He begins to teach about the lifestyle of the kingdom.

The entire first half of our Lord's earthly ministry is marked by this: his making inroads into the kingdom of darkness (by preaching, restoring, and instructing).

All of this comes to a high point, and a transition point, when Jesus asks the question (notice how he describes himself): "What are people saying about the Son of Man?" When Peter confesses that he is the Christ (God's anointed prophet, priest, and king), Jesus then explains what he has come to accomplish. He is building his church on enemy-occupied territory; not even the gates of Hades will be able to stop him![43]

What follows this statement leads us to another category of "Son of Man" sayings.

Category 2

The second category of Son of Man sayings focuses not just on the *incarnate* Son of Man establishing his kingdom but on the *suffering* Son of Man paying the redemption price for that kingdom.

The confession of Simon Peter is a climactic point, and a hinge, in the gospel story. The next paragraph in Matthew's Gospel begins: "*From that time* Jesus began to show his disciples that

---

[43] Matt. 16:13–18.

he must go to Jerusalem and suffer many things . . . and be killed, and on the third day be raised."[44]

Is it any wonder that Satan tried to resist him once again—this time through Simon Peter's saying, "Don't go to the cross, Jesus; and don't take me near it either"? That explains the Savior's vigorous response: "Get behind me, Satan!"

> Peter, you need to understand that what I've come to do is to fulfill the promise of Genesis 3:15. That is what it means for me to be the Son of Man. In order for all dominion to be given to me, my heel must be crushed in conflict with Satan. Wherever I build the church, the gates of Hades are always waiting to attack. There is no other way for me to go.

At the end of the wilderness temptations Satan had left Jesus. He had been overcome, but he was not yet finally vanquished. Thus Luke adds, in a somewhat sinister aside, "He departed from him until an opportune time."[45]

Now that "opportune time" had come. Peter had confessed that Jesus, the Son of Man, was the Christ—God's prophet, priest, and king.[46] But he did not yet understand that the Son of Man was also the Suffering Servant. He resisted the idea that in order to purchase dominion, the incalculable price of Christ's sacrifice of himself on the cross needed to be paid. He saw where the Son of Man was destined to go—to the Majesty on High, surrounded by clouds of glory. He did not understand that the pathway to glory leads first to Calvary. Jesus could have said to him, as well as to the two on the Road to Emmaus:

> O foolish ones, and slow of heart to believe all that the prophets have spoken! Was it not necessary that the Christ should suffer these things and enter into his glory?[47]

---

[44] Matt. 16:21.
[45] Luke 4:13.
[46] Matt. 16:16.
[47] Luke 24:25–26.

Isaiah captures the significance of this better than any other prophet. The fourth of Isaiah's Songs of the Servant begins: "Behold, my servant shall act wisely; he shall be high and lifted up, and shall be exalted."[48] That is exactly the picture of the Son of Man in Daniel 7, isn't it? But then Isaiah catches a glimpse of what lies behind this exaltation—the place where the Son of Man has been *before* he comes to the Ancient of Days in glory. That glory lies on the far side of his sufferings. He comes to the throne from the cross, where he "was marred beyond human semblance."[49]

Alec Motyer vividly captures the sobering nature of Isaiah's words here:

> The thought is not that the Servant suffered more than any other individual, or more than other humans but that he experienced disfigurement "from [being] an individual . . . from [belonging with] humankind," so that those who saw him stepped back in horror not only saying "Is this the Servant?" but "Is this human?"[50]

Jesus has to be marred beyond human semblance, to go down into the uncharted waters where, as he is covered in our sin, God no longer sees his own reflection in his Son. In that cold and dark place a kind of deep disintegration of being takes place. "The Proper Man" feels as if he is being un-manned! As he meditates on Psalm 22, does he pause on the words?[51]

> But I am a worm and not a man,
>   scorned by mankind and despised by the people.
> All who see me mock me;
>   they make mouths at me; they wag their heads[52]

---

[48] The four Servant Songs are Isa. 42:1–4 (some include vv. 5–9); 49:1–6 (some include vv. 7–13); 50:4–9 (some include vv. 10–11); 52:13–53:12.

[49] Isa. 52:14.

[50] J. Alec Motyer, *The Prophecy of Isaiah: An Introduction and Commentary* (Downers Grove, IL: InterVarsity, 1993), 425.

[51] The psalm that appears to have been on his mind during the latter part of his crucifixion.

[52] Ps. 22:6–7.

Jesus began to be . . . troubled," says Mark's account. He uses a rare verb to describe Jesus' experience.[53] J. B. Lightfoot notes that it

> describes the confused, restless, half-distracted state, which is produced by physical derangement, or by mental distress, as grief, shame disappointment.[54]

Even though we are fallen creatures, the Bible insists that we remain the image of God. We may be deformed. We may be twisted. The mirror in which God's image was originally reflected may be shattered. But we are still human. There is still some reflection of what we were meant to be. But in order to repair that, Jesus needs to go underneath, as it were; to experience this terrible sense of disintegration—to be treated as sin,[55] to bear the curse,[56] to become "a worm, and not a man" in order to bring about a new integration and a new humanity.

Common grace. In view of all he planned to do through Jesus, God continued to show his creation common grace. Even the most fallen people are permitted to enjoy privileges that God originally gave to his image bearer. Many criminals possess memorable abilities but twist them; unpleasant people have stable marriages and family life; the proud and arrogant have amazing natural talents. Thus the marred image of God continues to taste his blessing yet persists in rebellion against him. The daughter held in love on her father's knee slaps him in the face; the son is given gifts by his father but spits on him.

To bear the penalty of such rebellion, the Son of Man, "obedient to the point of death, even death on a cross,"[57] looked submissively toward his Father, longing to see his gaze of responding love—but everything was darkness. He felt utterly forsaken. Nature

---

[53] *Adēmonein*; see Mark 14:33.
[54] J. B. Lightfoot, *Saint Paul's Epistle to the Philippians* (London: MacMillan, 1913), 123.
[55] 2 Cor. 5:21.
[56] Gal. 3:13.
[57] Phil. 2:8.

itself seemed to empathize, and darkness came over the scene for three hours lest anyone pry into the mystery:[58]

> Well might the Sun in darkness hide
> And shut his glories in
> When God the mighty maker died
> For man the creature's sin.[59]

This description of the Son of Man as the Suffering Servant, wounded for our transgressions, bruised for our iniquities, emerges throughout the Gospel narrative. Here is the Son of Man on his way to being marred for us:

> Now the men who were holding Jesus in custody were mocking him as they beat him. They also blindfolded him and kept asking him, "Prophesy! Who is it that struck you?" And they said many other things against him, blaspheming him. When day came, the assembly of the elders of the people gathered together, both chief priests and scribes. And they led him away to their council, and they said, "If you are the Christ, tell us."[60]

But Jesus had only one thing left to say to them. Their time had come and gone.

> But he said to them, "If I tell you, you will not believe, and if I ask you, you will not answer. But from now on the Son of Man shall be seated at the right hand of the power of God."[61]

Now you see what Jesus is saying:

> I am that Son of Man described in Daniel. You humiliate me now, but it is I who will come to the Ancient of Days surrounded by his glorious angels in the clouds of heaven. I will receive domin-

---

[58] Luke 23:44.
[59] Isaac Watts, "Alas and Did My Savior Bleed," 1707.
[60] Luke 22:63–67.
[61] Luke 22:67–69.

ion. What you see now is my marring beyond human semblance. But this is going to purchase dominion beyond human imagination. The day will soon dawn when all authority in heaven and earth becomes mine! This too you will see![62]

The full flood of his suffering and passion follows. But something amazing is happening here. It is especially clear in Luke's Gospel. Two contradictory things seem to take place—and they do so again and again—as if the very narrative itself were crying out to us, "Don't miss the point! Do you see what is happening here?"

On five occasions—with a further occasion implied—Jesus is examined and then pronounced innocent. But then he is condemned:

> Pilate: "I find no guilt in this man." (Luke 23:4)
>
> Pilate again: "I did not find this man guilty." (Luke 23:14)
>
> The implication: "Neither did Herod, for he sent him back to us." (Luke 23:15)
>
> Pilate, yet again: "Why, what evil has he done? I have found in him no guilt deserving death." (Luke 23:22)
>
> The criminal on the cross: "We are receiving the due reward of our deeds; but this man has done nothing wrong." (Luke 23:41)
>
> The Roman centurion: "Certainly this man was innocent!" (Luke 23:47)

How can Jesus be declared innocent, repeatedly, and yet be condemned to death by crucifixion as though he were guilty?

Luke is surely saying: "Don't you see that God has written the gospel into the very heart of the experience of his Son at this point? The innocent is taking the place of the guilty, in order that the guilty might be treated as the innocent." This is underlined by the nature of the charges brought against Jesus. They were blasphemy in the religious court (a capital offense) and treason in the

---

[62] See Rev. 1:7.

civil court (also a capital offense). He was found "not guilty" on each count. Yet he was executed.

What is the underlying meaning of all this? It is very simple. The crimes are not his.

Whose crimes, then, are they?

Blasphemy and treason are the two crimes on our charge sheet in the judgment court of God. We have blasphemed against God by making ourselves the center of our world and the lord of our own life. We have committed treason against God's rightful authority by refusing his will. That was what Adam did. It is what we also have done.

Jesus has been found guilty and condemned for our crimes.

In the Gospel narrative, every reliable witness before the court points to Jesus and says, "He is innocent of these charges." There is only one possible explanation, therefore, for his death. He is accepting the charges leveled against us in the courtroom of the eternal Judge. He, the perfect image of God, is being marred beyond human semblance so that we might be restored to the image of God.[63]

This is a profound mystery. But it can also be stated so simply that a child can understand it:

> There was no other good enough
> To pay the price of sin;
> He only could unlock the gate
> Of heaven and let us in[64]

> Bearing shame and scoffing rude,
> In my place condemned he stood,
> Sealed my pardon with his blood:
> Hallelujah! What a Savior![65]

---

[63] See Rom. 8:29; Eph. 4:24; Col. 3:10.
[64] Cecil Frances Alexander, "There Is a Green Hill Far Away," 1848.
[65] Philip P. Bliss, "Man of Sorrows," 1875.

Category 3

This brings us to the final category of these Son of Man sayings. We have seen that:

- Jesus is the incarnate Son of Man who establishes his kingdom.
- Jesus is the suffering Son of Man who purchases his kingdom.

But now we must add a third dimension:

- Jesus is the triumphant Son of Man who will consummate his kingdom.

This is what Jesus has in view in the Great Commission:

> All authority in heaven and on earth has been given to me. Go therefore and make disciples of all nations.[66]

We tend to associate these famous verses with baptisms and missionary farewells. They are certainly relevant to both. But even more fundamentally these words are about Jesus' triumph as the Son of Man—without which both Christian baptism and world missions would be meaningless.

The words, "All authority on heaven and earth has been given to me," echo Genesis 1:26–28. Jesus is saying:

> I am the second Man, raised from the dead. I am the one who has paid the purchase price for a fallen world. I have bought it back at the cost of my death. And now that all dominion is mine and I am going back to my Father, I want you to begin to do spiritually what Adam was called to do physically: bring the gospel to the whole world; turn this wilderness back into a garden!

Amazingly—considering how cowardly and confused they once were—Jesus' disciples begin to do exactly that.

---

[66] Matt. 28:18–19.

Simon Peter (now a graduate of Jesus' forty-day seminar) preaches as an able biblical theologian. On the day of Pentecost he shows how the Scriptures point to Jesus Christ. He explains that Jesus has been exalted at the right hand of God and has asked his Father to fulfill his promise. Now, in order to bring the nations (and not just the Jews) to Christ, the Spirit is being poured out on all flesh. The rebellion of the tower of Babel is being reversed—people from many nations with different languages now all hear the sinner-uniting gospel simultaneously. The Son of Man is now sharing the kingdom of God with his saints in all the nations. The Abrahamic promise is being fulfilled; the messianic promise that the Son would inherit the nations is coming to fruition; the Suffering Servant is now highly exalted and causes kings to be silent in awe before him.[67]

And so the last days have begun and move on inexorably toward the final day. The Son of Man has come to the throne of the Ancient of Days. He is sharing the kingdom with the saints of the Most High. Now, together, we wait for the time when the triumph of the Son of Man will be visible everywhere.

The final actions of the Son of Man are described graphically by Paul in his great resurrection chapter, 1 Corinthians 15. It includes, but also looks beyond, the moment of the final resurrection. Paul sees the whole of human history in terms of two men, indeed two Adams—Adam and Christ.[68] He writes:

> Christ has been raised from the dead, the firstfruits of those who have fallen asleep. For as by a man [Adam] came death, by a man has come also the resurrection of the dead. For as in Adam all die, so also in Christ shall all be made alive. But each in his own order [notice the order]: Christ the firstfruits [i.e., he is the guarantee of the final harvest], then at his coming [the final har-

---

[67] See for these aspects of Christ's fulfillment of prophecy: Gen. 11:1–9; 12:1–3; Ps. 2:8; Isa. 52:13, 15; 53:12; Joel 2:18–20.

[68] "And why?" asks the great seventeenth-century theologian-pastor Thomas Goodwin, "because these two between them had all the rest of the sons of men hanging at their girdle." *The Works of Thomas Goodwin*, 12 vols. (Edinburgh: James Nichol, 1862), 4:31.

vest] those who belong to Christ. Then comes the end, when he delivers the kingdom to God the Father after destroying every rule and every authority and power.[69]

What would Adam have done if he had exercised his dominion and extended the garden to the ends of the earth?

Since he failed, we cannot give a dogmatic answer. But we may assume that he would have come to the throne of the Ancient of Days—as any father-honoring son would come to his own father—to say:

Father, I am finished. No weeds left. Flowers all over the place! Father, you gave this to me. Father, will you accept this garden as my love gift to you?

Imagine the mutual embrace that would have resulted.

Adam failed.

But, says Paul, on the final day Jesus, the Son of God, *in his capacity as Son of Man*, will take the kingdom he has purchased and come once again to his Father to say:

Here it is, Father; as the second Man, the Son of Man, I have saved and restored all this for you and for your glory. It is my love gift to you. I offer it to you on behalf of all those for whom I shed my precious life blood, who are now your adopted children.

That kingdom will include all who believe in Jesus.

We will all be spectators.

No, we will be more than that: we will all be participants.

But then hold your breath. For Paul goes on to say:

When all things are subjected to him, then the Son himself will also be subjected to him who put all things in subjection under him, *that God may be all in all*.[70]

---

[69] 1 Cor. 15:20–24.
[70] 1 Cor. 15:28.

Paul is not saying that God the Son will lose his significance. Nor is he denying that the Son is equal in dignity, power, eternity, and glory with his Father. Rather, he is speaking here of the Lord Jesus in his specific capacity as Son of Man. Incarnate in our humanity, he is our representative, mediator, substitute, savior, and king. He leads us to God's throne in worship. He is our spokesman to the heavenly Father. He will "come" then once more to the Father and say, "Father, it is all yours—on behalf of your redeemed people, I say, 'We want you to be all in all.' "

Picture in your mind's eye this scene. See the Son of Man as he comes to the throne of the Ancient of Days and kneels before him as our representative head and on our behalf. Then, in one glorious event, every knee will bow and every tongue will confess that Jesus Christ is Lord to the glory of God the Father.

Oh, to be there in that moment!

Oh, to see the Son honored by the Father!

Oh, to say, "Father, be all in all."

Then, surely, the kingdom and the power and the glory will be his—forever and ever, world without end.

In the light of this, it goes without saying that we need to think more about our Savior's glorious exaltation. But before we do that we must take a further look at him as the Suffering Servant.

6

Jesus Christ,
the Suffering Servant

The second half of the prophecy of Isaiah is set against the dark backcloth of God's judgment on his people and their exile in Babylon.[1] Slowly, out of the shadow lands, a figure appears. He is described by God as "my servant," and as we have seen, his presence dominates a series of poetic passages known collectively as the "Servant Songs."

The Fourth "Servant Song"

The fourth of these songs, Isaiah 52:13–53:12, is by far the best known. Here the servant appears as the Suffering Servant—a portrait that profoundly influenced the way in which the New Testament writers spoke of Jesus.[2]

The servant appears first of all as a glorious figure:

> Behold, my servant shall act wisely;
> > he shall be high and lifted up,
> > and shall be exalted.[3]

But then, inexplicably, the servant becomes a sufferer.

---

[1] From Isaiah 39 or 40 through 66.
[2] The United Bible Societies edition of *The Greek New Testament* lists seven quotations and thirty-four allusions and verbal parallels from Isaiah 52:13–53:12 found in the New Testament.
[3] Isa. 52:13.

As many were astonished at you—
>> his appearance was so marred, beyond human semblance,
>> and his form beyond that of the children of mankind—[4]

Then as the song continues the servant is portrayed as despised and rejected, a man of sorrows, familiar with grief. Then the truth begins to unfold. He is taking the place of others. He is suffering for them:

Surely he has borne our griefs
>> and carried our sorrows;
yet we esteemed him stricken,
>> smitten by God, and afflicted.
But he was wounded for our transgressions;
>> he was crushed for our iniquities;
upon him was the chastisement that brought us peace,
>> and with his stripes we are healed.
All we like sheep have gone astray;
>> we have turned—every one—to his own way;
and the Lord has laid on him
>> the iniquity of us all. . . .

Yet it was the will of the Lord to crush him;
>> he has put him to grief;
when his soul makes an offering for sin,
>> he shall see his offspring; he shall prolong his days;
the will of the Lord shall prosper in his hand.
>> Out of the anguish of his soul he shall see and be satisfied;
by his knowledge shall the righteous one, my servant,
>> make many to be accounted righteous,
>> and he shall bear their iniquities.[5]

Then once again he is exalted, and the connection between his humiliation and his exaltation is explained:

---

[4] Isa. 52:14.
[5] Isa. 53:4–6, 10–11.

Therefore I will divide him a portion with the many,
　　and he shall divide the spoil with the strong,
because he poured out his soul to death
　　and was numbered with the transgressors;
yet he bore the sin of many,
　　and makes intercession for the transgressors.[6]

Isaiah 53 was written under the direction of the Spirit of God. The author is speaking about something beyond his own experience. Yet at the same time, this is God's word in man's mouth,[7] and so the prophet describes what he sees within the limitations of his own psychology and his own humanity.

Questions at the Dinner Table

Imagine, if you will, Isaiah writing these words, and then at the end of the day going home to his family. As he spends time relaxing with them, one of his boys asks him, "Were you writing something today, Dad?"

All he could say, surely, would be something like, "Well, I wrote these words down:

Who has believed what he has heard from us?
　　And to whom has the arm of the Lord been revealed?
For he grew up before him like a young plant,
　　and like a root out of dry ground;
he had no form or majesty that we should look at him,
　　and no beauty that we should desire him.
He was despised and rejected by men;
　　a man of sorrows, and acquainted with grief;
and as one from whom men hide their faces
　　he was despised, and we esteemed him not.[8]

---

[6] Isa. 53:12.
[7] A typical Old Testament way of describing prophecy; cf. Jer. 1:9.
[8] Isa. 53:1–3.

What if someone else in the family then asked: "Exactly what does that mean? Who were you writing these words about? Is it someone you know?"

Isaiah could only reply, "You know, I can't say properly. Although I was sitting writing, inwardly I felt as if I was standing on my tiptoes looking over the horizon, peering into future history. I was asking these very questions myself, wondering, even trying to imagine, who this person could possibly be and how all this will unfold."

That is not merely conjecture. Peter says that while the angels find themselves wondering about what it is like for believers to experience the grace of God in the gospel, the prophets were wondering "what person or time the Spirit of Christ in them was indicating when he predicted the sufferings of Christ and the subsequent glories."[9]

We are blessed to be able to read our Bibles from back to front. The explanations of the New Testament allow us to understand passages from the Old. They help us to see how everything points to the Lord Jesus. In particular it sees these words of Isaiah fulfilled.[10]

So against this backdrop—Christ seen as the Suffering Servant—let us, as it were, follow Jesus as far as we can into his passion.

The Suffering One

What does it mean that Jesus was "the *Suffering* Servant"? To answer that question—even in part—we need to try to follow Jesus, on the evening of his crucifixion, to the garden of Gethsemane.

> And he came out and went, as was his custom, to the Mount of Olives, and the disciples followed him. And when he came to the place, he said to them, "Pray that you may not enter into temptation." And he withdrew from them about a stone's throw, and knelt down and prayed, saying, "Father, if you are willing, remove this cup from me. Nevertheless, not my will, but yours,

---

[9] 1 Pet. 1:10–12.
[10] See, for example, Matt. 8:17 (Isa. 53:4); John 12:38 (Isa. 53:1); Acts 8:32–33 (Isa. 53:7–8); 1 Pet. 2:22 (Isa. 53:9).

be done." And there appeared to him an angel from heaven, strengthening him. And being in an agony he prayed more earnestly; and his sweat became like great drops of blood falling down to the ground. And when he rose from prayer, he came to the disciples and found them sleeping for sorrow, and he said to them, "Why are you sleeping? Rise and pray that you may not enter into temptation."[11]

Earlier, in chapter 1, we found ourselves in a garden. Here we visit another garden. It is a familiar garden to Jesus and his disciples, the garden of Gethsemane.[12] It is actually an olive grove. But on this particular night it is the center of the universe and stands at the crossroads of history.

A Unique Description

The New Testament contains no physical description of Jesus. Despite the books you may have had in childhood with pictures of Jesus, you know they were an attempt on the part of artists to come up with a way of portraying him—usually in a very traditional Western way. But those pictures are not derived from any information we are given in the Bible.

Here, however, in Gethsemane, we are given a rare moment of insight. It is truly a description—but into the emotional life, the mental state, the psychology of the Lord Jesus as he faces the cross. Here we are shown the depths of his humanity in a way we otherwise would never see.

Each of the first three Gospels provides us with an emotions-piercing portrayal of what Jesus experienced. The sight is deeply disturbing. For now Jesus, who made such calm predictions about his coming suffering and all that he would endure at the hands of cruel and wicked men, now expresses himself in "loud cries and tears."[13]

---

[11] Luke 22:39–46.
[12] Jesus went there frequently with his disciples; John 18:2.
[13] Heb. 5:7.

Some twenty-one years have elapsed since that day in the temple precincts when Jesus said to Mary and Joseph that he must be in his Father's house.[14] On that occasion his earthly parents did not really understand what he was saying. They must have gone back down the road, saying, "What do you think Jesus meant by saying, 'Don't you know that I need to be in my Father's house?'?" Did Joseph say to Mary, "Well, you're his mom; don't you understand what he meant? What do you think?" Did she say, "Well, I'm still thinking about it all. I'll reflect on it again. I have been storing up his words and pondering them deeply"?

Later on when Jesus tells his disciples—and not for the first time—that he must go up to Jerusalem, they still didn't really grasp what he was saying:

> "We are going up to Jerusalem, and everything that is written about the Son of Man by the prophets will be accomplished. For he will be delivered over to the Gentiles and will be mocked and shamefully treated and spit upon. And after flogging him, they will kill him, and on the third day he will rise." But they understood none of these things. This saying was hidden from them, and they did not grasp what was said.[15]

They were as close to him as anyone could possibly be. They had heard all his preaching and witnessed his miracles. And yet here we find them—and they still do not understand what he was talking about. The meaning of it all is hidden from them.

Now, we are not to be so presumptuous as to say, "My, my! I think if I'd been there, I'd have understood it perfectly. I can't believe these disciples. Not the brightest bunch after all! Poor fellows. Jesus told them this on a number of occasions. How hard is this really to understand? 'I am going up to Jerusalem. I will suffer. I will die at the hands of cruel men.'"

---

[14] Luke 2:41–52.
[15] Luke 18:31–34.

How could they possibly reconcile all this talk about suffering with the wonderful Master they followed? How could they hold together the idea of a king who would out-king all the kings, who was also a priest who would bring a final sacrifice of infinite value, with a prophet who would permanently banish their ignorance? Yet, despite the unpalatable nature of what Jesus said, his meaning was unmistakable. They simply could not take it in.

Humble Approach

If we're honest, we see the same thing in ourselves. That is why we should appreciate the hymn that has as its refrain:

> Oh, make me understand it,
> Help me to take it in,
> What it meant for thee, the Holy One
> To bear away my sin.[16]

Such understanding—so that the gospel makes a real impact on our lives—comes only as a result of God's grace and his goodness to us. In the face of so much mystery, we need to learn to think prayerfully and properly when we come to a passage like this. We need to ask, what exactly is happening here?

It is also all too possible for us simply to be emotionally stirred by this scene without actually wrestling with its inner meaning or its implications. We then end up responding to the sufferings of Christ in a way that is little more than sentimental.

Here, in Isaiah's description of the Suffering Servant, we encounter statements like this: "It was the will of the LORD to crush him; he has put him to grief."[17] What do these statements mean?

They are all unfolded in the crucifixion, which is now being anticipated by Christ in this garden. It all seems such a mess—a

---

[16] Katherine Kelly, "Give Me a Sight, O Savior," 1944.
[17] Isa. 53:10.

horrendous mess: Jesus, the faithful Servant, is about to be crucified between two criminals on a garbage heap outside the city walls
of Jerusalem—betrayed, denied, deserted, spat upon, flogged, de-
meaned. How is it possible for the purpose of God to be at the
heart of all this? How can Isaiah say—however reverently—that
God is in control of it all, that it "was the will of the Lord to
crush him"?

Paul explains: Jesus was made a curse for us, so that we might
receive God's blessing in him.[18] Why was he made "a curse" for us?
Because "he made him to be sin who knew no sin, so that in him
we might become the righteousness of God."[19] The letter to the
Hebrews helps us again: Jesus "made propitiation for the sins of
the people";[20] he became the sacrifice that exhausts God's wrath
against our sin.

In Gethsemane Jesus is anticipating offering himself as a "vi-
carious" or "substitutionary" atonement sacrifice for our sins.

Unless we appreciate the notion of substitutionary atonement,
the New Testament's teaching on the death of Christ will be en-
tirely incomprehensible to us—at best it will become a tragedy of
misguided heroism.

We will return to that. For the moment there are three straight-
forward, but important, observations we need to make.

Compassion

As we view Christ through a biblical lens and see him as Suffering
Servant, our first reaction is likely to be: "What compassion is here!"

Think of Christ's circumstances as he goes into the garden.
Notice his first thought. It is not for himself but for his followers.
He turns his attention to these young men he had called and pa-
tiently taught, with whom he has lived, and whom he loves far more

---

[18] Gal. 3:13.
[19] 2 Cor. 5:21.
[20] Heb. 2:17.

than they could ever begin to imagine (as John put it: "Having loved his own who were in the world, he loved them to the end"[21]).

Look at the selflessness of Jesus. "I am among you as one who serves," he had said.[22] And now especially, as the extremity of the situation begins to crush him, he continues to serve the interests of his disciples.

Notice how lovingly he urges them to maintain close communion with the Father lest they fall into temptation: "Watch and pray that you may not enter into temptation."[23]

Earlier, when he had spoken to Peter, it must have been with a breaking heart:

> Simon, Simon, behold, Satan demanded to have you, that he might sift you like wheat, but I have prayed for you that your faith may not fail.[24]

The first "you" in that statement is in the plural form. But the second "you" is singular. "Simon," Jesus says, "Satan has asked to sift you. Not just you, Simon, but all of you. All of you are going to go through the grinder. All of you are going to be stretched to the breaking point by the events that are about to unfold. But, Simon, you need to know that I have prayed especially for you."

Some of us, whenever the slightest thing goes wrong, have no time for anything or anyone else. Perhaps that is mainly true of men? Our wives have a phenomenal capacity for endurance and for keeping going. But the slightest thing goes wrong with some of us men and we go into retreat—and we expect others to come and minister to us!

But that's not Jesus. Despite all that he faces—and all that he sees written on the faces of these disciples—he cares, and he says,

---

[21] John 13:1.
[22] Luke 22:27.
[23] Mark 14:38.
[24] Luke 22:31–32.

"I am praying for you particularly." He knows that they will be tempted to doubt him and to desert him and even deny him.

The same spirit of loving concern runs through his great prayer in John 17, which should be read alongside the narrative of the Synoptic Gospels. *Here* Jesus tells the disciples to pray that they will not fall into temptation. *There*, in John's Gospel, he prays for them that they will be kept strong in the coming time of temptation.[25] The goal of the Suffering Servant's prayers is that they will be kept so that they may be able to pray for themselves to be kept!

The perseverance of these disciples in this extremity will not happen by chance. Nor does it happen simply by *divine fiat*. It happens by God's grace, a grace that is mediated to them through God-given means.

Ordinary Means of Grace

This is an appropriate point to remind ourselves of a dimension of Christian living that is increasingly ignored. We need a better appreciation of what we often call the "ordinary means of grace."

What are they? Prayer, preaching, the fellowship of God's people, the ordinances of baptism and the Lord's Supper, the experience of trials, and so on. So when Scripture says, "Keep yourselves in the love of God,"[26] it implies that God brings to completion the good work that he has begun *by working in us and through us*.[27] We are kept by God as we also keep ourselves resting in him.

A second feature of Jesus' ministry is present here.

Commitment

The Gospels tell us that as Jesus entered the garden of Gethsemane, he told eight of the disciples to remain at one particular spot, perhaps as guards. He then took three of them (Peter, James,

---

[25] John 17:11.
[26] Jude 21.
[27] Phil. 1:6; cf. 2:12–13.

and John) deeper into the garden. Then he himself went further in and began to pray.[28]

What then?

Luke describes his posture: he "knelt down."[29]

Earlier in his Gospel, Luke described the posture of a Pharisee at prayer. He was "standing."[30] Jews usually did (as did Christians for many years in church services). But Jesus is not standing in the posture of formal prayer. No, he kneels down—at least at first. Matthew records that he then "fell on his face"[31] and Mark that he "fell on the ground."[32] There is an intense urgency here, even desperate need—and yet it is coupled with submission as Jesus prostrates himself in the dust before his Father. There is an inevitability about this strong emotion. Jesus is about to move from the theoretical, as it were—the long-held knowledge that crucifixion and the judgment of God await him at the end of the road—to the imminent and the actual.

Facing major surgery is perhaps the closest most of us ever come to this. The date is in your diary. In the meantime you are constantly meeting people in the daily thoroughfare of life and responding to their questions: "Yes, they're going to take me in at 8:00 a.m., and then they'll do this. At 9:00 a.m. they'll do this, and at 11:00 a.m. they'll do that." We say to ourselves, "At about half past three in the afternoon I'll be eating jelly and ice cream"—all the while hoping we'll manage to come out at the far end of the operation.

But then the actual morning dawns.

You can't get saliva in your mouth.

The sterile environment sweeps over you.

Now you pray in a different way . . .

[28] Luke 22:41.
[29] Luke 22:41.
[30] Luke 18:11.
[31] Matt. 26:39.
[32] Mark 14:35.

At the Crossroads to the Via Dolorosa

Christ kneels; then he falls to the ground; then he lies face down on the ground, prostrated in prayer before his Father. The apostle Paul did not see this happen. But he knew what it meant. Jesus is becoming obedient unto death, even death on a cross.[33]

Our Lord's outward posture here is expressive of the passion within.

Think of what it must have meant for him to speak to his Father in this way: "Father, if you're willing, take this cup from me. Yet not my will but yours be done."

Somewhere in the vastness of the economy of God in eternity, the Father, the Son, and the Holy Spirit entered into a covenant. Reducing it to its simplest terms, each of them committed himself to completing a particular aspect of our redemption. All three persons would always be involved in everything God was doing. But the Father would plan salvation, the Son would come to procure it, and the Spirit would be sent to apply it.

The Son came on his saving mission. He chose to come to our fallen world from the endless and undiluted glories of life in heaven. From the intimacy of the heaven where he had everlastingly tasted the pleasures of intimate fellowship with his Father within the community of the life of God, he now comes into this morally and spiritually polluted world. He is born through a natural birth canal; he grows physically, and in favor with God and man.[34] He learns from Joseph how things work in the carpenter's shop, and so on. But all the time there is a sense that his life is moving inexorably to a date that God has marked in the divine calendar. Until then Jesus' "hour" or "time" had not yet come.[35]

Now, here, in the garden of Gethsemane, Jesus' hour has

---

[33] See Phil. 2:8.
[34] Luke 2:52.
[35] John's Gospel is punctuated with such references. See 2:4; 7:30; 8:20; cf. 12:23; 13:1; 17:1.

come—and it coincides with what he calls the "hour" of the "power of darkness."[36]

The hour hand was now moving inexorably toward midnight on the face of the divine clock of destiny. Jesus has his clearest preview yet of the agonies that are before him. Is it not safe to say that here he experiences a hellish onslaught? Here, surely, the malicious hosts of the world of darkness are unleashed against him, assaulting his psyche, oppressing him to the core of his being. The distant prospect has come near in all its gut-wrenching reality.

Jesus must have been aware of what crucifixion looked like, perhaps even what it sounded like, and of what it did to a man. How often had he thought to himself that it would be like the pictures of suffering recorded in Psalm 22: roaring lions tearing their prey, strong bulls surrounding him.

But tonight was different. Now forethought and imagination were giving way to reality. Now here come the powers of hell!

Jesus is almost beside himself with horror. Hardly surprising then that Martin Luther comments, "No one has ever been so terror stricken by death as he was. . . . He felt and experienced death's throes more than all of us together."[37]

Mark tells us that while he was still with the disciples he "began to be greatly distressed and troubled." That's the point of his words: "My soul is very sorrowful, even to death."[38] This, as we have seen, is language that expresses the kind of feeling of distraction that is the result of a profound shock.

Peter, James, and John now see Jesus in a new light. They had seen him before, as the rabbi teaching, and as the prophet proclaiming the word of the Lord. They had seen him as the compassionate one with little children on his knee. They had seen him in the

---

[36] Luke 22:53.
[37] Martin Luther, *The Complete Sermons of Martin Luther*, vol. 5, ed. Eugene F. A. Klug (Grand Rapids, MI: Baker, 2000), 384.
[38] Mark 14:33–34.

exercise of his authority over the wind and the waves. But they had never seen this before.

Did one of them perhaps say to him, "Jesus, are you feeling all right? Is there something wrong?" Our Lord responded, "My soul is overwhelmed with sorrow." He doesn't say, "You know, I'm feeling a little off-color today. I'm not feeling so good this evening— I'm just not my usual self somehow." No, he says, "My soul is overwhelmed."

Jesus is now going through an unprecedented experience. It is even more terrifying than the overwhelming fear the disciples experienced in the boat in the Galilean storm. They had cried to him: "Jesus, wake up! We're drowning! Save us! Don't you care if we perish?"[39] But Jesus is alone in this boat as it sails into the storm of divine wrath. Now the symbolism of his water baptism at Jordan into his people's sins is being fulfilled in the reality of his baptism in blood at Calvary. Now, in a climactic water judgment, all God's waves lash upon him and his billows overwhelm him as he makes his people's sins his possession:[40]

> Save me, O God!
>   For the waters have come up to my neck.
> I sink in deep mire,
>   where there is no foothold;
> I have come into deep waters,
>   and the flood sweeps over me.
> I am weary with my crying out;
>   my throat is parched.
> My eyes grow dim
>   with waiting for my God.
> More in number than the hairs of my head
>   are those who hate me without cause;
> mighty are those who would destroy me,

---

[39] See Mark 4:35–41.
[40] Ps. 42:7.

> those who attack me with lies.
> What I did not steal
> > must I now restore?[41]

In his holy humanity, Jesus recoiled from the awfulness of the humiliation, suffering, and death that awaited him.

He asked to be "saved." "Father, if you are willing, remove this cup from me."[42]

If he had not done so, he would have been less than truly human. He would not be human or holy (would he?) if the reality before him was a matter of relative indifference. He had never before tasted the awful reality that now faced him—the Father's wrath falling on his holy soul. The prospect was unimaginable.

Fully and Truly Human

The story of the church's understanding of the person of Jesus Christ is one of swings and roundabouts. The pendulum swings between diminishing the divinity of Jesus and diminishing his humanity. In the last 150 years, liberalism has diminished Christ's divinity, and orthodoxy, partly in reaction, has run the risk of diminishing his humanity. In our insistence that Jesus is Lord, that he is the divine King—which we unreservedly affirm—we must never fall into the error of having a less than human, or more than human, Christ. If we do, we reduce his saving work to a mathematical formula, and, worse, we have a Christ who is not able to be a savior.

But if our Savior is truly and fully human, then his work is a flesh-and-blood reality. He is a real man in this real garden among real friends who fail him just when he is facing this real onslaught. On the one hand, that onslaught comes from hell (was there ever fiercer temptation than now?). "Turn away from obedience to death, even death on a cross." On the other hand the cup he shrinks

---

41 Ps. 69:1–4.
42 Luke 22:42.

from drinking contains an onslaught from heaven.[43] It will bring him eventually to the point of crying out, "My God, my God, why have you forsaken me?"

Jesus knows this is what it will mean if he is to suffer and die as an atoning sacrifice for sin. He is about to taste God-forsakenness.

A Savior Who Felt and Feels

There is a mental dimension to this suffering. It has an intellectual aspect. There is also a psychosomatic aspect. Jesus is engulfed by the emotion of the occasion. He had repeatedly asserted the divine necessity of his suffering. But now he is imminently confronted by the ordeal. On an evening cold enough for a fire to be kindled in the courtyard of the high priest, his sweat presses out of his body like great globules of blood and drops down to stain the ground.[44] How do you sweat like that on an evening so cold that Peter will soon want to warm himself by a fire?[45]

Some of us know mental anguish. Some of us even feel it to the point where we fear for our sanity, and even for our lives. Some are plagued in mind by fears and feel ourselves at times on the verge of despair and hopelessness.

Does the gospel have anything to say to us here?

It does indeed! It tells us that Christ has been touched with all this, on the inside. Do you know that the Lord Jesus understands what it is to be overwhelmed? It is not for nothing that the New Testament writer who says:

> In the days of his flesh, Jesus offered up prayers and supplications, with loud cries and tears, to him who was able to save him from death, and he was heard because of his reverence. Although he was a son, he learned obedience through what he suffered,[46]

---

[43] For indications of this as the significance of the "cup" see Ps. 75:8; Isa. 51:17, 22; Jer. 25:15–17; Ezek. 23:32–33; Hab. 2:16.
[44] Luke 22:44.
[45] Luke 22:55.
[46] Heb. 5:7–8.

also wrote that

Jesus Christ is the same yesterday and today and forever.[47]

These last words are not a description of the immutable eternal nature of the Son. That is a biblical truth but not the truth of this text. For this statement tells us that *Jesus still is all that Jesus once was during the course of his ministry.* Jesus' vast sympathy, his compassion, his perfect understanding of suffering both mental and physical—all so vividly portrayed in the Gospels—is still as real today as it was yesterday. More—he will always be like that! He is still today the very same person who is described in the Gospel narrative—and all for us!

There is a physical aspect to this suffering. That bears saying. There is little need for elaboration, is there? Crucifixion is, surely, the most brutal, cruel, and unnatural punishment ever devised by man. We need to be clear that there was nothing in Christ's humanity to blunt his emotions or to anaesthetize him to lessen his suffering. The horrific way the death penalty passed on him was carried out—despite all his innocence—is not part of a novel. It was reality.

Indeed, so concerned was Jesus to suffer in unrelieved fashion that when offered wine mingled with gall as an anaesthetic to deaden his senses and to alleviate his suffering, he declined.[48] He will drain the cup of suffering to its very dregs.

There is a social dimension to his suffering. You may never have thought that this could be of any real significance for Jesus. But think about it now. Jesus was friendly. Jesus didn't go through his ministry as a rock or as an island.

Jesus didn't build walls—he built bridges; he gathered people around him. Children loved him. Distinguished people came to him. Ordinary people listened to him. His friends were important

---

[47] Heb. 13:8.
[48] Matt. 27:34.

to him. He loved his neighbors. He was affectionate. He enjoyed human relationships.

So it is not a small matter for Jesus, as he kneels down in this garden (formerly a place of tranquility and friendship for him), that he is about to be marginalized, isolated, and condemned. His companions of three years are about to betray him, deny him, or demean and desert him. No friendly face. No hand to hold. No whispered word of encouragement.

Jesus is about to be abused by the religious establishment he had sought to treat with honor and respect. He is about to be publicly exposed to humiliation—a humiliation that, surely, his dearest friends and closest family also felt deeply. Jesus, who bows down in the garden, is about to die unjustly, alone, with his friends standing at best at a distance from him until near the end. Did he even feel that those who were most important to him in this earthly life thought *he* was letting *them* down?

So, you see, if you've got only an exclusively divine Jesus, you will tend to think, "Well, what about it? He's the Son of God. That's not an issue with him."

Yes, it is.[49]

When we were both growing up in Glasgow, Scotland, various groups of Christians used to visit from the United States. They would bring singers and all sorts of songs for us to learn—some of which deeply impressed even youngsters' minds and hearts. One of them was the song that began,

> There were ninety and nine that safely lay
> In the shelter of the fold.
> But one was out on the hills away,
> Far off from the gates of gold.
> Away on the mountains wild and bare.

---

[49] Perhaps we should point out here that this would not only be to ignore our Lord's humanity; it would be to misunderstand his deity also.

Away from the tender Shepherd's care.
Away from the tender Shepherd's care.

"Lord, Thou hast here Thy ninety and nine;
Are they not enough for Thee?"
But the Shepherd made answer: "This of Mine
Has wandered away from Me;
And although the road be rough and steep,
I go to the desert to find My sheep,
I go to the desert to find My sheep."[50]

Written by Elizabeth Clephane, it was always sung to the tune written by Ira D. Sankey. It was very dramatic. These first two verses seemed to roll along with the tune. But with the third verse we began to feel the darkness fall. We were beginning to lose sight of where Jesus had gone. We knew we could not go all the distance with him.

But none of the ransomed ever knew
How deep were the waters crossed;
Nor how dark was the night the Lord passed through
Ere He found His sheep that was lost.
Out in the desert He heard its cry,
Sick and helpless and ready to die;
Sick and helpless and ready to die.

Then the fourth and fifth verses seemed to describe all that we were allowed to know:

"Lord, whence are those blood drops all the way
That mark out the mountain's track?"
"They were shed for one who had gone astray
Ere the Shepherd could bring him back."
"Lord, whence are Thy hands so rent and torn?"

---

[50] Elizabeth Clephane, "The Ninety and Nine," 1868.

"They are pierced tonight by many a thorn;
They are pierced tonight by many a thorn."

And all through the mountains, thunder riven
And up from the rocky steep,
There arose a glad cry to the gate of Heaven,
"Rejoice! I have found My sheep!"
And the angels echoed around the throne,
"Rejoice, for the Lord brings back His own!
Rejoice, for the Lord brings back His own!"

None of us knows the bitter chill of these waters, the depth of this darkness. The Lord was in a place all on his own in Gethsemane. We can look long on this scene and do our best to understand it. But we can never fully comprehend it. This is where we are grateful for Paul's words:

> For this reason I bow my knees before the Father . . . that according to the riches of his glory he may grant you to be strengthened with power through his Spirit in your inner being, so that . . . you, being rooted and grounded in love may have strength to comprehend with all the saints what is the breadth and length and height and depth, and to know the love of Christ that surpasses knowledge.[51]

Another hymn—this time Welsh—comes to mind:

Here is love, vast as the ocean,
Loving kindness as the flood,
When the Prince of Life, our Ransom,
Shed for us His precious blood.
Who His love will not remember?
Who can cease to sing His praise?

---

[51] Eph. 3:14–19.

He can never be forgotten,
Throughout Heav'n's eternal days.[52]

In fact, Jesus' extremity in the garden is so great, his suffering so deep, that an angel is commissioned from heaven to minister to him. (Are not angels "ministering spirits sent out to serve for the sake of those who are to inherit salvation"?[53])

Can you imagine the summons that goes out for this angel?

"I have a visit for you," says the Father. "I want you to go down to Jerusalem, to the Mount of Olives—and more specifically to the garden of Gethsemane. There you will find him."

"Who, Lord?"

"My Servant. There you will find the Suffering One. He is my Son. Minister to him."

Who can describe, far less explain, the nature of that angel's ministry? Alexander Whyte, the nineteenth-century minister of Free St. George's Church in Edinburgh, said that when he reaches heaven, after he has met Christ himself, the person he wants to meet more than any other was this angel.

Surely you understand that? Alexander Whyte presumably didn't know how to exegete this particular verse. But perhaps when all things are made clear, and he—and we—no longer see through a glass darkly—perhaps then something of the answer will be ours.

Of course, once the angel comes (so we think)—all will be well, won't it? You might think so, judging by some current books on the angelic. When an angel comes, everything is wonderful . . . isn't it?

Is it?

After the angel came, things were far from being wonderful.

Notice the striking statement that follows: "And there ap-

---

[52] William Rees, "Here Is Love, Vast as the Ocean," 1876.
[53] Heb. 1:14.

peared to him an angel from heaven, strengthening him. *And being in an agony he prayed more earnestly*."[54]

Our Lord must surely have been grateful to God for the ongoing strength given from heaven. But it did not lessen the intensity of his struggle. It simply made it possible for him to continue it to the end. (Notice, incidentally, that Jesus did not "draw down" some special power from his deity at this point—his deity and humanity are never confused, or compounded, in this way. Rather, he received help from his Father through the visit of an angel.)

Donald Macleod underlines the poignancy of all this when he writes:

> In these things Christ still stands beside those who are emotionally overborne, finding their grief and bewilderment insupportable and likely to be fatal.[55]

What compassion. What commitment!

We must consider one further dimension in which the Lord Jesus is the Suffering Servant.

Contrast

At last Jesus rises from prayer.

Now the wrestling is over.

In contrast to his earlier prostration, Jesus now returns calmly to his disciples.

Now he is ready to walk the Via Dolorosa.

Now there is no doubt that he will go down this path of suffering to its end.

Now everything he has anticipated in these dark moments in the garden will become reality.

The angel has come. He has strengthened him. He is on his feet.

---

[54] Luke 22:43–44.

[55] Donald Macleod, *From Glory to Golgotha* (Fearn, Ross-shire: Christian Focus, 2002), 88.

He has endured Gethsemane. He returns to his disciples. They—despite his exhortation to watch and pray—have fallen asleep. But he has taken the cup into his hands; he will now raise it to his lips.

Luke very graciously says that the disciples were exhausted from sorrow. But perhaps he is not just being gracious. Luke was a physician. He was interested in the nature of Jesus' sweat. Perhaps he is giving us an insight. These young men were caught up in an overwhelming experience. They couldn't bear it, either. The wonderful thing, of course, is that Jesus addresses them one more time: "Why are you sleeping? Let me give this to you once more. Here's what you need to do. Get up and pray so that you will not fall into temptation."

Then, as the soldiers come with Judas to arrest Jesus, he steps out in front and says, "I presume you're looking for me." There is no cowering here; there is no running, no hiding.

It was partly in the light of this intense passion of the Savior that Martin Luther developed his deep concern about the state of the church in his day. It had become materially strong and was awash with its own sense of power, glory, and triumphalism. It had what Luther called a *theologia gloriae*—a theology of glory, its own glory. What it needed was a *theologia crucis*—a theology of the cross.

It is this theology of the cross that we find here. God grant that in seeing Christ as the Suffering Servant we will be done once and for all with the superficial triumphalism that sadly emanates from too many Christian organizations and churches.

Have you ever considered the fact that on the average Sunday, pastors minister to congregations of people whose lives are marked—and often marred—by quiet desperation? Sadly, some churches, and the finance-seeking "ministries" that sprout in abundance, have become very skilled at masking all this with promises of victory and a life beyond the reach of pain and sorrow.

Masking tape to cover deep needs is always a profoundly unhelpful and unrealistic antidote for broken hearts. Using it betrays a deeply unbiblical—and indeed ultimately cruel—theology. And, sadly, the broken and overwhelmed and shattered and sordid and sad are never pointed to the Suffering Servant, who will love them, sympathize with them, save them, and graciously and gradually transform them.

Our churches will have all too little ministry to the least and last, the lost and left out, until we are prepared to acknowledge that Christ himself was a suffering servant who entered into the depths of our humanity. We *therefore*, as followers of Jesus, albeit still sinners, must be suffering servants also.

Our smiles of superficial triumph repel rather than attract those who are wrestlers with the troubled sea of life. The silly affirmations of God's intervention in our lives taking us beyond the realm of trial and difficulty, the sort of testimony to the work of Jesus that seems to suggest that if you are a Christian in a hurry, then all the traffic lights will go in your favor, or that your daughters will be pretty, or that your sons will be handsome and get the best jobs, or that you will always gets A's on your test—*all this is demolished by the biblical gospel.* Christians are indeed winners, but the prize is waiting on the other side of suffering.

How could we ever imagine it would be different, when our Lord and Savior came as a suffering servant?

A Suffering Savior for Outcasts

Think of the untouchable community at the bottom of the traditional caste system in India, the vast numbers of people who are Dalits by birth. They live without hope. They are the offscouring. They are the wounded. They are the unemployable. Then someone goes and tells them of Jesus, of a Savior who was despised and rejected by men, a Master who was a man of sorrows, familiar with grief—that Jesus Christ is the Son of God from whom people hid their faces—as though he belonged to the Dalit caste!

The Dalit responds: "We never knew there was such a person. Who is this?" Is it any wonder that many of these people are attracted to Christ?

This is all very different from some American Christianity, isn't it? Or some Australian, or some British, or some South African Christianity. Here the appeal is to the quarterback, to the TV personality, to the cheerleader, to the business success. But we didn't get that from our Bibles. It is time to be done with all this if, in the twenty-first century, we are going to be able under God to bring the gospel to the needy and marginalized.

We want a Jesus who does all the suffering, don't we? As A. W. Tozer said, prophetically, years ago, "We want to be saved but we insist that Christ do all the dying. No cross for us, no dethronement, no dying. We remain king within the little kingdom of Mansoul and wear our tinsel crown with all the pride of a Caesar; but we doom ourselves to shadows and weakness and spiritual sterility."[56]

But what do you find in the Gospels? This: after Jesus tells the disciples, "The Son of Man must suffer many things and be rejected by the elders and the chief priests and the scribes and be killed," he tells them: "If anyone would come after me, let him deny himself and take up his cross and follow me. For whoever would save his life will lose it, but whoever loses his life for my sake and the gospel's will save it."[57]

In the same way, by the time Paul is wrapping things up and writing his final letter to Timothy, he urges him: "Share in suffering for the gospel by the power of God. . . . Share in suffering as a good soldier of Jesus Christ."[58]

Yes, the servants of the Suffering Servant must suffer with him. It is the pathway to glory.

So, today, if you hear God's voice, do not harden your heart.[59]

---

[56] From *The Root of the Righteous*, in *Gems From Tozer* (Carlisle, UK: Send the Light Trust, 1969), 20.
[57] Mark 8:31–37.
[58] 2 Tim. 1:8; 2:3.
[59] Heb. 4:7.

7

Jesus Christ,
the Lamb on the Throne

Probably the most well-known of the paintings of Gaugin, the French impressionist painter, is hanging in the Boston Museum of Fine Arts. On the upper left corner of the canvas he wrote in French: "Where do we come from? What are we? Where are we going?" The Bible answers each of these questions and leaves us in no doubt about our origin or our end.

Despite the clarity with which the Bible speaks, vast numbers of men and women have been deceived by the Evil One about both their beginning and their ending. Inevitably, they become confused about both their past and their future. In the great cities of the world as well as in the vast hinterlands that stretch far away from the major centers of world population, men and women search for meaning.

This issue is, of course, a matter of interest to the academic community—sociologists, psychologists, and others. But it is more frequently, and often with greater poignancy, tackled in the arts.

Some years ago the one-woman play *The Search for Signs of Intelligent Life in the Universe*, written by Jane Wagner, was running on Broadway. It starred Lily Tomlin.

Lily reflects on her life. At one point she stops and says, "I worry where tonight fits in the Cosmic Scheme of things." And then she adds, "I worry there *is* no Cosmic Scheme to things."[1]

---

[1] Jane Wagner, *The Search for Intelligent Life in the Universe* (New York: Harper Collins, 1987), 26.

It's Peanuts-cartoon funny. But it has a sharp edge.

Einstein, in his *Credo*, wrote:

> Our situation on this earth seems strange. Every one of us appears here involuntarily and uninvited for a short stay without knowing *the whys or the wherefores*.[2]

Who would have thought that Einstein would have language in common with the popular British singer Petula Clark—and vice versa? She sang in the sixties:

> You wander around on your own little cloud,
> and you don't see the *why or the wherefore*.

Her advice?

> Don't sleep in the subway, darlin'
> Don't stand in the pouring rain.[3]

Is that all that can be said?

It is against this background that the gospel brings a message of glorious hope. Part of that message is found in Revelation, the final book of the Bible. It constantly affirms this central biblical truth: the history of our world is ultimately defined by salvation history. Indeed, history itself cannot be properly read and understood without biblical lenses.

In Revelation we find John, its author, on the small island of Patmos, just off the coast of modern-day Turkey. He has been banished there because of his faithfulness to the gospel. He describes himself to those to whom he writes as "your brother and partner in the tribulation."[4] His first readers are believing people, who, like

---

[2] Originally written in 1932 and recorded for the benefit of the German League of Human Rights.
[3] "Don't Sleep in the Subway," Tony Hatch and Jackie Trent. The emphases in this quote and the previous from Einstein's *Credo* are ours, in order to highlight the remarkable harmony between the words of a recognized genius and the words of the pop culture of the 1960s.
[4] Rev. 1:9.

ourselves, are trying to make sense of their lives. In particular, in their case in the first century, they are trying to reconcile their own very testing circumstances with the message of Christ's victory over sin, Satan, and death.

These Christians had heard the gospel preached to them. They would have listened to sermons like the one Peter preached on the day of Pentecost. Empowered by the Holy Spirit, he had given a panoramic view of history. He had made it clear to his hearers that the Jesus about whom he was speaking was the one who had been crucified, had died, and was buried. But God had raised him from the dead. He had appeared to his disciples. Now he was ascended to God's right hand. The outpouring of the Holy Spirit was the visible evidence of his invisible enthronement. All this was simply in accordance with the Scriptures.

These first-century believers understood that their ascended Lord and King was now the one who was fully in control of all circumstances. He, as we saw earlier, is the one in whom "all things hold together."[5] They were anticipating an ultimate, defining moment in which the fullness of all that God had planned would finally be completed, and the lordship of Christ would be established throughout the whole earth once and for all.

These Christians would have been able to affirm all the articles of the Apostles' Creed.[6] They believed them. But the real difficulty was that much they affirmed did not seem to be happening—particularly the gospel promises of the triumph of God and of the victory of his kingdom.

John's fellow apostle Simon Peter had already written that "scoffers" would come during the "last days"—an expression that refers to the era between the first coming of Jesus in his incarnation and his final return in power and glory. During this period Chris-

---

[5] Col. 1:17.
[6] We are not implying that the Apostles' Creed was already in its present form in the latter years of the first century, but simply that its affirmations were basic elements of the "faith that was once for all delivered to the saints" (Jude 4).

tians should anticipate that these scoffers—people who follow their own devices and desires—will say: "Where is the promise of his coming? You're saying Jesus Christ is a triumphant King, and a returning Lord. Well, where is he? Everything seems to be the same this year as it was last year and the year before."[7]

In one sense, of course, the scoffers had a point. What the Christians had anticipated had not fully come. They were the church, the bride of Christ, the followers of Jesus. But they were insignificant in their society. They were a small group—one or two additions now and then but nothing of great significance. Meanwhile when they looked at the world around them, they saw the empires of man seemingly growing in influence. In particular they were growing in their ability to aggravate these followers of Jesus. Soon, in powerful and manipulative ways, they would be viciously persecuting them. Emperor worship was flourishing, and those who refused to affirm that Caesar was lord and who thus refused to deny their Lord Jesus would be liable to the death penalty.

It is not hard to imagine that in the average Christian family, perhaps sitting at the family meal, the dinner conversation would turn to these threats. A son or daughter might say:

> Well, what is this Christian life after all? How does this work? Is this just a private thing, Dad? Can we take this out into the community? Does it have an impact in the Roman Empire? What do we do with this? Where is Jesus? I thought you said Jesus was coming back. Will he be coming back soon?"

Although Christians confessed Jesus as Lord, it must have seemed to many of them that Caesar was still lord. To how many of them did the Evil One come—as a liar and the father of lies[8]—and insinuate into their minds, "You know what? You have probably simply bought into the great delusion. You get on fine as long as you're in

---

[7] See 2 Pet. 3:3ff.
[8] John 8:44.

your group, singing your songs. But when you get off on your own and think about it . . . well, not a lot has changed, has it?"

Says Leon Morris:

> To a church perplexed by such problems Revelation was written. It was sent to a little, persecuted, frustrated church, one which did not know what to make of the situation in which it found itself.[9]

That is a hugely important perspective to have on the book of Revelation. It is not a kind of theological Rubik's Cube. It was not written as an intellectual puzzle for a group of people who enjoyed solving mathematical problems. Not for a moment. Its first readers were in too much of a life-and-death situation to enjoy that kind of relaxation.

But, you say, "Well, that's all well and good, but we're a long way removed from that, aren't we? We are not threatened by emperor worship in America!"

But our lives are set against the backdrop of a world in turmoil: economic gloom, human deprivation, a world at war on multiple fronts, rampant immorality. We waken in the morning to a steady dose of news that could drive us to despair. And it never stops. Yes, the decisions that are made by politicians in Washington, in Beijing, in London, in Kabul, in Cairo, in Jerusalem, and in Delhi have far-reaching effects on lives. But we also know that we are caught up in global realities too enormous for us to understand and predict, far less control. And we realize that those who say they know don't understand how little they know. For all the security systems we have, personally and nationally, insecurity abounds in our modern society.

Few twentieth-century songwriters can match the ability of Paul Simon to convey this sense of futility and angst with such clarity and pathos. In our world reality is broken.

So how does Jesus transform this understanding of reality?

---

[9] Leon Morris, *Revelation: An Introduction and Commentary* (London: Tyndale, 1969), 20.

Enter the Book of Revelation

Sometimes we find ourselves asking, is there any way in which we can go behind the scenes of all of this? Is there anyone who can give us an inkling of where we're going and what we're doing?

Well, is there?

Here we have it! This is exactly what happened to John one Lord's Day on the island of Patmos.

He was taken behind the scenes of time and history. "I was in the Spirit," he says, "and I heard behind me a loud voice like a trumpet."[10] One commentator cleverly notes that John is not taken to some *never-never land*, but instead he is taken into the *ever-ever land* of God's eternal values and judgment.

Soon, in chapter 4, he is standing before a higher throne than any known in this world. It is occupied—by God!

There is a scroll in the palm of God's right hand. It has writing on both sides, but it is sealed with seven seals. A summons is issued throughout the cosmos to find someone who can break the seals and open the scroll.

But almost immediately everything John hoped to see comes to a grinding halt.

He has been assured that he would be given an insight into the unfolding purposes of God. The curtain will be pulled back to enable him to see into the mysteries of God so that he can write to encourage the beleaguered saints of his day—to reassure them with the message of the victory of God. But let John tell the story in his own words:

> And I saw a mighty angel proclaiming with a loud voice, "Who is worthy to open the scroll and break its seals?" And no one in heaven or on earth or under the earth was able to open the scroll

---

[10] Rev. 1:10.

or to look into it, and I began to weep loudly because no one was found worthy to open the scroll or to look into it.[11]

What is he to do now?

"No one was found."

John meant "no one on Patmos," didn't he?

No.

Well, perhaps "here on earth?"

No.

"No one on earth or under the earth was able to open the scroll or look into it."

Well, then, one of the mighty angels, or archangels, or cherubim, or seraphim could surely open the book?

No.

"No one in heaven . . . was able to open the scroll or to look into it." This is not a matter of brute strength; it is a matter of being "worthy" to do it.

So John tells us, "I wept and I wept because of this." But then,

one of the elders said to me, "Weep no more; behold, the Lion of the tribe of Judah, the Root of David, has conquered, so that he can open the scroll and its seven seals."[12]

"Weep no longer, John!" says one of the twenty-four elders around the throne. "There is a mighty Lion able to do this."

There is no doubt about the identity of this lion. He is "the Lion of the tribe of Judah, the Root of David." It is the Messiah promised in the Old Testament Scriptures,[13] the conquering king, the Son whom God has appointed to reign on Zion's holy hill. The nations will be given to him as an inheritance.[14] His enemies will

---

[11] Rev. 5:2–4.
[12] Rev. 5:5.
[13] Gen. 49:9–12.
[14] Ps. 2:6–8.

become a stool for his feet.[15] Neither death nor hell, neither Satan nor sin will prevent his triumph. In him the purposes of God will be finally and triumphantly fulfilled.

God has provided in Jesus the solution to John's tears. "Weep no more"! But then John turns to look—

> and between the throne and the four living creatures and among the elders I saw a Lamb standing, as though it had been slain, with seven horns and with seven eyes, which are the seven spirits of God sent out into all the earth. And he went and took the scroll from the right hand of him who was seated on the throne.[16]

John expects to see the Lion of the tribe of Judah. That was indeed the great messianic expectation. But John's theological vision is better here than it had been when, perhaps in his teenage years, Jesus had called him to follow him. Now he sees what John the Baptist had first seen: the Lion of the tribe of Judah conquered by becoming "the Lamb of God, who takes away the sins of the world."[17]

This is the only way anyone ever sees the Lion King—we come to know and trust him only as he comes to us in the form of a slain lamb. It is only in Christ crucified that we find the answer to all the alienation and the dislocation to which sin has led. That is why what follows is the only possible appropriate response:

> And when he had taken the scroll, the four living creatures and the twenty-four elders fell down before the Lamb, each holding a harp, and golden bowls full of incense, which are the prayers of the saints. And they sang a new song, saying,
>
> Worthy are you to take the scroll
>   and to open its seals,

---

[15] Ps. 110:1.
[16] Rev. 5:6–7.
[17] John 1:29.

> *for you were slain, and by your blood you ransomed people*
>   *for God*
> *from every tribe and language and people and nation,*
> and you have made them a kingdom and priests to our God,
>   and they shall reign on the earth.[18]

We do not need Christ to tell us that our world is full of trouble. But we do need his triumph over the sources of our troubles if they are not to perplex and overwhelm us. This is why the book of Revelation is such good news. From this point onward it strikes this wonderful, triumphant, encouraging note: the Lamb King has triumphed. He is able to unlock the seals and unfold the mystery.

Two Titles

The Triumphant One has two great titles.

One—the Lion—goes back to Jacob's dying prophecy about an individual who would come through the line of his son Judah—a lion-like figure who would reign, and whose reign would be marked by a divinely given abundance.[19]

This is the only occasion in the book of Revelation when the Lion is mentioned. (The Lamb is mentioned twenty-nine times.) But although it does not recur, clearly "Lion" is what Jesus is throughout the book. It abounds with illustrations of his power, victory, and authority.

The Lion is also "the root of David." That description goes back to the promise given to David that from his seed the Messiah King would come. But that promise requires further interpretation, which it is given in Isaiah and Jeremiah.[20] Christ is both the Lord of, and the branch from, David! The Messiah comes after David, but he was in fact David's Lord and was therefore before him. This was

---

[18] Rev. 5:8–10.
[19] Gen. 49:9–12.
[20] Isa. 11:1–2; Jer. 23:5–6.

the testimony of Psalm 110:1–2, the passage that Jesus reminded the Pharisees had tied them in knots trying to interpret:[21]

> The LORD says to my Lord:
>   "Sit at my right hand,
> until I make your enemies your footstool."
>
> The LORD sends forth from Zion
> your mighty scepter.
> Rule in the midst of your enemies!

How could David's son be his Lord? Only if the "son" is the Lord Jesus—the one who is both of the seed of David and at the same time the eternal Son of God.

But John looks and sees a lamb. His vision is filled with a tapestry-like presentation of the humility of Christ. Here is the one who was obedient to his Father, even to the point of submitting to death on a cross.[22]

The book of Revelation is like a paint-by-numbers set. A painting of a quality far beyond that of the ordinary child's ability emerges as the young artist fills in the numbered outline with the corresponding numbered colors from the paint palette provided.

Similarly in Revelation, John "paints" above his ability as the Spirit helps him. In the case of this book, however, the "paint palette" is full of Old Testament texts. John's mind is a palette saturated in Scripture. As he paints these scenes for oppressed Christians, his description is composed of Bible verses, allusions, prophecies, and so forth. The entire atmosphere of this tapestry has the aroma of the Old Testament being fulfilled in Christ.

We cannot be absolutely certain how well John's first readers knew the Old Testament. But some of them must have been quite

---

[21] Matt. 22:41–46.
[22] Phil. 2:8.

familiar with much of its teaching.[23] So, when this picture of the Lamb was placed front and center, their minds would quickly have gone to the events of the Passover, recorded in Exodus 12. They knew that God's exodus deliverance came through the sacrificed Passover Lamb.[24] They must also have thought of Isaiah 53 with its description of the Suffering Servant who was "like a lamb that is led to the slaughter."[25] This is the Lamb whom John sees—the "Lamb, standing as though it had been slain."

But he is no longer *slain*. He is *standing*! He is alive with resurrection life and power.

But notice something else. It is still obvious that he once had been slain; his wounds are still visible. The wounds remind us of the costly death by which our redemption has been achieved; the fact that this slain Lamb *stands* reminds us of the triumph of his resurrection.

When you see this in your mind's eye, don't you want to sing with the host of heaven? Or at least sing with the church on earth in the presence of Christ about

> Those wounds, yet [still] visible above,
> In beauty glorified:

> Crown Him with many crowns, the Lamb upon His throne.
> Hark! How the heavenly anthem drowns all music but its own.
> Awake, my soul, and sing of Him who died for thee,
> And hail Him as thy matchless King through all eternity.

> Crown Him the Lord of life, who triumphed over the grave,

---

[23] If Paul's approach during his ministry in Ephesus (one of the churches to which Revelation was sent, Rev. 1:11) was typical of early-church ministry, many early Christians must have been saturated with biblical teaching. Paul taught in the hall of Tyrannus every day of the week (Acts 19:9) for a period of some two years. Some manuscripts of the text of Acts suggest he did this during siesta time, 10.00 a.m. until 3.00 p.m. (see footnote in the ESV). If so, Paul gave some of the first readers of Revelation a seminary education in biblical studies and theology!

[24] It is surely significant that when Luke records the conversation Jesus had with Moses and Elijah on the Mount of Transfiguration, he notes that they discussed Jesus' "departure" (Gk. *exodus*); Luke 9:31.

[25] Isa. 53:7.

And rose victorious in the strife for those He came to save.
His glories now we sing, who died, and rose on high,
Who died eternal life to bring, and lives that death may die.

Crown Him the Lord of peace, whose power a scepter sways
From pole to pole, that wars may cease, and all be prayer and
      praise.
His reign shall know no end, and round His piercèd feet
Fair flowers of paradise extend their fragrance ever sweet.

Crown Him the Lord of love, behold His hands and side,
Those wounds, yet visible above, in beauty glorified.
No angel in the sky can fully bear that sight,
But downward bends his burning eye at mysteries so bright.

Crown Him the Lord of years, the Potentate of time,
Creator of the rolling spheres, ineffably sublime.
All hail, Redeemer, hail! For Thou hast died for me;
Thy praise and glory shall not fail throughout eternity.[26]

But there's still more in this tapestry of Jesus. The Lamb, you notice, has "seven horns and . . . seven eyes, which are the seven spirits of God sent out into all the earth."[27]

These words, read in a group study, can be just like red meat to a lion! Many a home Bible study is derailed when you come to a little sentence like this—"seven horns and seven eyes," and so on. And before you know it, Mrs. Jenkins immediately wants to tell everyone all about the seven horns—and suddenly the big picture of who Jesus is disappears in a discussion of Russia, or China, or the European Economic Community. This is the point at which the firm and wise leader asks Mrs. Jenkins to go make the tea and coffee! She should never have bought that big book that gave so much detailed explanation of how contemporary world history is

---

[26] Matthew Bridges, "Crown Him with Many Crowns," in *The Passion of Jesus* (1852).
[27] Rev. 5:6.

minutely described in Revelation but said so little about the sheer glory of the Lord Jesus! It can be all very fascinating and wonderful, like sudoku, or math. But it can take you deep into the night.

No, God is much simpler than all that. The horns speak of power and majesty; the eyes remind us that Christ has sent his Holy Spirit into the world, with all of his omniscience, perfect understanding, and wonderful discernment. And the fact that there are seven horns, eyes, and spirits simply expresses numerically the idea of fullness and perfection.

It would be a great pity to have been shown this vivid picture of the Father seated on the throne, the Son in all his redeeming grace and glory, and the Holy Spirit in all the fullness of his saving ministry but see only horns, eyes, and numbers! That would be to obscure what is plain and clear and to marginalize what is central.

Actually, there is a litmus test for interpretation written into the text here. It is this: what effect does this vision have on me? Perplexity? Debate? Calculation? All wrong responses. For the response of heaven is this:

> The four creatures and the twenty four elders fell down before the Lamb, each holding a harp, and golden bowls full of incense, which are the prayers of the saints. And they sang a new song, saying,
>
> "Worthy are you to take the scroll
>   and to open its seals,
> for you were slain, and by your blood you ransomed
>   people for God
>   from every tribe and language and people and
>   nation."[28]

This is the song of redemption. John is identifying its cost: the price was the blood of the Lamb being shed. On Calvary Christ once and

---

[28] Rev. 5:8–9.

for all purchased our redemption. That is why later, in Revelation 7, another picture will emerge in the vision. One of the elders asks John a question (was it the same elder he heard earlier?[29]):

> Do you see this innumerable multitude of people standing before the Lamb, all clothed in white? Do you know who they are and why their robes are so white?

John said what you and I would say, didn't he?

> Sir, you know. You tell me, please.

The elder countered:

> You know who they are, John. They're believers who have come out of the great tribulation. They have washed their robes and made them white in the blood of the Lamb.

Who are these people? They are believers cleansed from their sins by the shed blood of the Lamb and now clothed in his perfect righteousness.

Perhaps if we read the book of Revelation more with our eyes fixed on the Lord Jesus, we would be more enthusiastic about some of the older hymns. Here is another we sing all too rarely:

> With harps and with viols, there stands a great throng
> In the presence of Jesus, and sing this new song:
> *Unto Him Who hath loved us and washed us from sin,*
> *Unto Him be the glory forever, Amen.*

> All these once were sinners, defiled in His sight,
> Now arrayed in pure garments in praise they unite:
> *Unto Him Who hath loved us and washed us from sin,*
> *Unto Him be the glory forever, Amen.*[30]

---

[29] Rev. 5:8.
[30] A. T. Pierson, "With Harps and with Viols, There Stands a Great Throng," n.d.

The Lamb of God who takes away the sin of the world is enthroned at the very center of this picture. He is the epicenter of the unerring plan of God's redemptive strategy.

As people are drawn around this scene, they recognize first that here we have our Redeemer, the one who has saved by substitution. This is the gospel. It is also the message of Revelation 4 and 5.

> O perfect redemption the purchase of blood,
> To every believer the promise of God.
> The vilest offender who truly believes
> That moment from Jesus a pardon receives.[31]

A Thief at Heaven's Door

Think of the two thieves crucified on either side of Jesus.

They both seemed at first to have vented their pain and anger on him.[32] But then one of them becomes silent. Soon he speaks: "Don't keep saying these things! We are here because we deserve to be on a cross. But this man has done nothing wrong." And then, turning to Jesus in penitential recognition, he says with such humility, "Jesus, remember me when you come into your [OT "you"] kingdom."[33]

Witnessed by the angels in glory, at a cost beyond his or our ability to fathom, that thief reached the portals of heaven.

He had never had a church membership interview. There was no time. But can you—using your imagination—hear an interviewing angel asking him the vital questions?

Angel: Have you been justified by faith?

Thief: Well, I am not sure what that means. I don't think I have ever heard that expression before.

Angel: Well, I'll have to go get one of my supervisors, because there may be a problem here.

---

[31] Fanny J. Crosby, "To God Be the Glory," 1875.
[32] Matt. 27:44.
[33] Luke 23:40–42.

More questions. But then the issue is resolved when the thief speaks again:

> Thief: All I know is that I was on the cross at Jesus' side. I was guilty, I was in agony, I was dying, and I was angry. And of all things, I heard people talking about him—saying he had claimed to be the Messiah. Well then, I thought, get us out of this mess! But I watched him and listened to him. Then I heard some of them spit out the word "Savior," and it dawned on me: this man had done nothing wrong. He was dying because of other people's sins.
>
> It just hit me, I don't quite know how: he is the Messiah, but he's dying because of other people's sins. And his name is Jesus—and I knew that meant "Savior." So I turned to him, knowing there was nothing I could do to pay back the debt of my sins, and I asked him, "Jesus, will you bring me into your kingdom? Would you be my Savior; would you be my sin bearer? Would you be the Lamb of God who takes away my sin?"
>
> And Jesus said to me, "Today you will be with me in Paradise."[34] The only reason I am here is that Jesus was on the middle cross. I know he died for sinners. And he promised me I could come into his kingdom.

What are you going to say on that day? The thief gave the only answer that opens heaven to us: "Jesus died for me." As a result, he was there—somewhere in the multitude in John's vision who heard the words:

You were slain, and by your blood you ransomed people for God.[35]

Notice the implication of these words: "You *ransomed* people *for God. Ransomed* means "purchased, bought into new ownership."

Is this an aspect of the gospel we have grasped clearly, first in

---

[34] Luke 23:43.
[35] Rev. 5:9.

our thinking and then in our living? We have been *purchased*. "You are not your own," writes Paul, "for you were bought with a price. So glorify God in your body."[36]

Well, do you?

A Vast Multitude

The heavenly song in Revelation 5 also underlines the scope of Christ's work of redemption. The cost of it is the blood of the Lamb; the scope of it is awe-inspiring. He has purchased men from God "from every tribe and language and people and nation."[37] This is the immense, expansive movement of God's saving work throughout the world. There are no geographical or ethnic limits.

Remember the moment Peter finally recognized this, when Jesus sent his Spirit to the Gentiles in the house of the Roman general Cornelius?[38] The full meaning of the Great Commission and the gift of the Spirit at Pentecost—and all the implications of his own sermon on that day—came home to him at last. Abraham was promised that in his seed the nations would be blessed; the messianic King would receive the nations for his inheritance; the Suffering Servant would sprinkle many nations.[39] "Now I get it," Peter said. "I know now that God does not have favorites. There is no favored-nation status."

The message of the gospel now goes into the whole world. Our friends—from our churches and many others too—are there, painstakingly working on the translation of the Scriptures among the Indians of Guatemala and in the Andes, in Mexico, and among primitive tribes in villages of the world that are on no map, with names we cannot spell, speaking languages we do not recognize, and using words we cannot pronounce.

---

[36] 1 Cor. 6:19–20.
[37] Rev. 5:9.
[38] Acts 10:1–48.
[39] Gen. 12:1–3; Ps. 2:8; Isa. 52:12.

Why? Because from all eternity God planned to bring to faith in Christ, and ultimately to glory, a vast multitude whom no man can number. And he has specified the way and the means by which he will accomplish it.

Paul understood that, when he said, "How are they to hear without someone preaching? And how are they to preach unless they are sent?"[40]

Christ sends us out into the neighborhoods, the workplaces, the institutions of our society, into the coffee shops, and into daily interaction with the warp and woof of life with a story to tell the nations.

Christians have a story unlike any other story.

Islam has only scales, the good outweighing the bad. Hinduism at best hopes for multiple reincarnations. Zen Buddhism has no real god at all. But we have this amazing story of Christ for which so many believers have been willing to be marginalized, persecuted, and even killed.

"Yes," says John, "there will be suffering and persecution. But there is something you should know, my dear Christian friends. I have gone through a doorway that opened into heaven. I have had a look behind the curtain. Here is what I have to tell you: there is before the throne of God an innumerable company of men and women and boys and girls who have been redeemed by the blood of the Lamb!"

"Oh," we say, "but we thought it said in Revelation 7 that there were only 144,000!"[41]

Don't you see that all of these numbers are symbolic? Are you looking at pictures and symbols as if they were the things themselves? No, there are 144,000 because that is the square of twelve (it isn't accidental there were twelve tribes) multiplied by the cube of ten. It is a kind of "perfect number" of enormous proportions. Not a single one will be missing! It isn't 143,999! For Jesus has told

---

[40] Rom. 10:14–15.
[41] See Rev. 7:4.

his Father: "Father, I have kept them all. I have done what you asked me to do. And not one of them is missing."[42]

Then as John looks he sees "a great multitude that no one could number."[43] They are like the sand of the seashore, the stars in the night sky, an innumerable company from every tribe and people and nation and language.

What a glorious, exhilarating reminder to us of the expansive and universal appeal of the gospel and the extent of the work of redemption accomplished by the Lamb upon the throne!

Sheer Privilege

In addition to the immense price and vast scope of our redemption, there is one further implication: the sheer privilege we have in experiencing that redemption. John hears a choir composed of the four living creatures plus the twenty-four elders now singing the closing words of their anthem of praise for the redeemed:

> You have made them a kingdom and priests to our God,
>   and they will reign on the earth.[44]

Then it seems the entire angelic population of heaven joins in, "myriads of myriads and thousands of thousands,"[45] now with another song of praise to the Lamb. And they are joined by the cosmic choir, "every creature in heaven and on earth and under the earth and in the sea, and all that is in them,"[46] singing, in effect:

> To God be the glory, great things he has done;
> So loved he the world that he gave us his Son,
> Who yielded his life an atonement for sin,
> And opened the life gate that all may go in.

---

[42] See John 17:12.
[43] Rev. 7:9.
[44] Rev. 5:10.
[45] Rev. 5:11.
[46] Rev. 5:13.

> O perfect redemption, the purchase of blood,
> To every believer the promise of God;
> The vilest offender who truly believes,
> That moment from Jesus a pardon receives.[47]

What a glorious reality this is—heavenly worship! There is plenty to do. It will be wonderful. If we move on to Revelation 7, which in many ways parallels the praise of Revelation 5, what do we find? This great multitude is singing God's praises and serving God's purposes.[48] The saints in glory are before the throne of God, and they serve him day and night in his temple. They are under the spreading protection of his wonderful care: "He who sits on the throne will shelter them with his presence."[49]

What is the result of all this? "They shall hunger no more, neither thirst anymore."[50] They are perfectly satisfied with God's provision. And then John adds a beautiful little footnote with a little bit of poetic license in it: the Lamb who was slain for them has now become the Shepherd who leads them:

> The Lamb in the midst of the throne will be their shepherd,
>   and he will guide them to springs of living water,
> and God will wipe away every tear from their eyes.[51]

Here it is, then—God's final answer to all our alienation and dislocation. Here is the answer to the angst of our generation and of every generation.

Who else can wipe away every tear from our eyes? Who else can enter into the depths of our circumstances and deal with them? Who else can supply living water so that we will never thirst again? Only Jesus. Only the one who is the Lamb of God.

---

[47] Fanny Crosby, "To God Be the Glory."
[48] Rev. 7:12, 15.
[49] Rev. 7:15.
[50] Rev. 7:16.
[51] Rev. 7:17.

If, at one sitting, you read Revelation 5 through 7, you will notice that this tapestry, which has the Lord Jesus at its center, surrounds him with an ever-expanding circle of praise:

- The four living creatures and the twenty-four elders worship him. (5:9)
- Myriads of myriads and thousands of thousands of angels worship him. (5:11)

But there is more to come. Much more:

- And I heard every creature in heaven and on earth and under the earth and in the sea, and all that is in them, saying: "To him who sits on the throne and to the Lamb be blessing and honor and glory and might forever and ever!" (5:13)

One of our favorite fellow countrymen is the great seventeenth-century theologian, preacher, and writer Samuel Rutherford. Here is what he has to say about this:

The Lord stands in no need of a testimony of such a worm as I. Although should the whole world be silent, the very stones would cry out. Yet, is it more than debt that I should confess Christ before both men and angels.

It would afford me unspeakable satisfaction were the throne of the Lord Jesus exalted above the clouds, the heaven of heavens, and on both sides of the sun. That I by his grace might put my seal, poor as it is, to the song of those, who with a loud voice sang, "Thou art worthy to take the book and to open the seals thereof." For thou wast slain and hast redeemed us to God by thy blood.

Blest were I could I but lay my ear of faith and listen to the psalms sung by the many angels round about the throne, and the beasts, and the elders, and the ten thousand times ten thousands, and thousands of thousands who, with a loud voice, sang, "Worthy is the Lamb that was slain, to receive power and

> riches and strength and honor and glory and blessing," and if I
> heard every creature in heaven and on earth and under the earth
> and such as are in the sea as John heard them saying, "Blessing
> and honor and glory and power be ascribed to him who sitteth
> on the throne and to the Lamb forever and ever."[52]

Here is this elderly man with a pen and a sheet of paper, and he
writes down his soul on it. What a testimony to the glory of Christ!

Two hundred years later, Anne Ross Cundell Cousin was so
deeply moved by Samuel Rutherford's *Letters* that she wove many
of his statements into a single nineteen-verse hymn, "The Sands
of Time Are Sinking." If it is sung at all now, it is the five- or six-
verse version that is used. The hymn has a particularly memorable
stanza that begins,

> The Bride eyes not her garment, but her dear Bridegroom's face.

Every minister who has conducted weddings knows that this is
true—no matter how much the bride's father spent on his beloved
daughter's wedding gown; no matter how much she had it adjusted
on the evening before the wedding; no matter how many attendants
had it perfectly arranged two minutes before she came down the
aisle. We are yet to see a bride preoccupied with her gown as she
walks down the aisle to stand beside the man she loves. No, she has
eyes for one man only.

> The Bride eyes not her garment, but her dear Bridegroom's face;
> I will not gaze at glory but on my King of grace.
> Not at the crown he giveth but on his pierced hand;
> The Lamb is all the glory of Immanuel's land.

One day the shadows will flee away. The days of preparation
will all come to an end. The final day will dawn. Already we ac-

---

[52] Samuel Rutherford, *A Testimony to the Covenanted Work of Reformation from 1638 to 1649 in Britain and Ireland*, Still Waters Revival Books, http://www.swrb.com/.

knowledge that Jesus is Lord. But then we will know him as we have never done before—in face-to-face fellowship. Then we will be made like him, for we shall see him as he is.[53]

We shall then see Jesus as the Seed of the Woman who crushed the Serpent's head, as the Prophet of God whose word directs our lives, as the Great High Priest who intercedes for us, and as the King who subdues all our enemies and reigns over us forever. We will recognize him as the Son of Man seated beside the Ancient of Days, and as the Suffering Servant who is now exalted as the Lamb on the throne.

On that day we will see with unclouded vision why his Father has given him the

Name above All Names.

---

[53] 1 John 3:2.

Subject Index

Scripture Index